# SIMPLIFY YOUR
# Household

A **Reader's Digest Simpler Life**™ Book

Designed, edited, and produced by Weldon Owen

THE READER'S DIGEST ASSOCIATION, INC.

**Executive Editor, Trade Books** Joseph Gonzalez

**Senior Design Director, Trade Books** Henrietta Stern

**Project Editor** Candace Conard

**Project Art Director** Jane Wilson


WELDON OWEN INC.

**President** John Owen

**Publisher** Roger S. Shaw

**Series Editor** Janet Goldenberg

**Copy Editors** Lisa R. Bornstein, Gail Nelson


**Art Director** Emma Forge

**Senior Designer** Elizabeth Marken

**Production Designer** Brynn Breuner

**Design Assistant** William Erik Evans

**Icon Illustrator** Matt Graif


**Production Director** Stephanie Sherman

**Production Manager** Jen Dalton


**Project Photographers** Chris Shorten, Brian Pierce

**Photo Stylist** JoAnn Masaoka Van Atta

**Photo Editor** Anne Stovell

A Reader's Digest/Weldon Owen Publication

Copyright © 1998 The Reader's Digest Association, Inc. and Weldon Owen Inc.

Library of Congress Cataloging in Publication Data

Aronson, Tara.
    Simplify your household / Tara Aronson.
      p.   cm.
    Includes index.
    ISBN 0-7621-0066-4
    1. Home economics.   2. Time management.   I. Title.
    TX147.A76   1998
    640—dc21                            98-9190

Printed in China

*A note on weights and measures: Metric equivalences given for*
*U.S. weights and measures are approximate. Actual equivalences may vary.*

# SIMPLIFY YOUR
# Household

## TARA ARONSON

Illustrations by TRAVIS FOSTER

Reader's
Digest

The Reader's Digest Association, Inc.
Pleasantville, New York/Montreal

# CONTENTS

## INTRODUCTION

YOUR HOME: SIMPLE TRUTHS

**6**

## EVERYTHING IN ITS PLACE

MAKING SPACE FOR WHAT'S IMPORTANT

**10**

## REDEFINING HOUSEWORK

FREEING YOURSELF FROM HOUSEHOLD
DRUDGERY

**30**

## COMING CLEAN

MAKING SHORT WORK OF HOUSECLEANING

**48**

## FIGHTING THE WASH-DAY BLUES

EXPERT TIPS FOR LIGHTENING YOUR LOAD

**66**

## MAINTENANCE AND REPAIR

KEEPING YOUR HOUSEHOLD
RUNNING SMOOTHLY

**78**

## SAFE AT HOME

SIMPLIFYING HOUSEHOLD
SAFETY AND SECURITY

**96**

## EASY HOME DECORATING

FAST FACE-LIFTS AND ARTFUL ADDITIONS

**112**

## CHECKLISTS AND RESOURCES

INFORMATION FOR HOUSEHOLDERS

**129**

## INDEX

**144**

Turning your house into a well-run
home is easier than you think.

# Your Home: Simple Truths

\*———\*———\*

There's nothing complicated about creating an inviting, efficient, and well-run home. And the truth is that it doesn't have to take endless hours with a mop and bucket, or some advanced degree in building maintenance, to keep your home and its systems running smoothly. All you need are a few simple techniques and a plan for prioritizing your tasks to make light work of household chores.

Everything you need to know about cleaning, organizing, and repairing what you can around your house—and calling in professional help if and when you need it—is included in this easy-to-use book. I'll tell you which chores you can safely skip now and then, and which ones are absolute musts for a clean and safe home. Whether your goal is to save time, to stretch your household budget, or to make running a home less stressful, you'll find the answers in this book.

I've gleaned much of the information offered in *Simplify Your Household* from my years of interviewing experts in virtually every aspect of household cleaning, maintenance, safety, and decorating for my articles in the *San Francisco Chronicle*'s "Home" section. Some of the techniques I've discovered have worked well in my own home, whereas others have been ineffective or too time consuming. In these pages you'll find the ideas that work best for busy folks like me—people who want a safe, presentable home, yet whose work and family life leave little time to do anything beyond the essentials. Whether you're looking for strategies on saving money on decorating, routine maintenance to keep small problems from becoming disasters, or last-minute tidying for unexpected guests, I'm confident that these ideas will work well in your home, too.

To help you pluck solutions and hints from these pages in the most efficient manner, I've packaged many of them in boxes and illustrated lists that quickly show you the simple solutions for decorating, storage, and more. In addition, at the back of the book you'll find helpful checklists you can use over and over again to keep your home running efficiently.

Yes, you *can* clean, maintain, and beautify your home in minutes, not hours. And this book is the first step toward achieving your cleaner, safer, lovelier, and more hassle-free home. There's never been a better time—or a simpler way— to streamline your household and your life.

Tara Aronson

On close inspection, any house can use more cleaning and fixing up.
The trick is to do only those jobs that are truly essential.

# Simple Symbols

❋

I F YOU'RE LOOKING FOR QUICK WAYS to save money, cut your labor time in half, or simply preserve your sanity, check out the tip boxes scattered throughout this book. In each box you'll find many easy-to-implement, less-stress solutions designed to help you run a household that's simply more enjoyable to come home to. Here's a complete guide to what the identifying symbols for each box mean:

**Labor Savers** are the last word in doing the job fast—and doing it right. In these boxes you'll find strategies to help you get your home cleaner, keep it running more smoothly, and have it look terrific—all with less work than you'd think.

**Time Savers** help you make the most of each and every precious moment. These tips will show you how to shave minutes—and sometimes hours—from your regular home-maintenance routines while maximizing the results of your efforts.

**Bright Ideas** are clever solutions to all kinds of household dilemmas—from hiding living-room clutter in a hurry to lifting lint from your newly washed clothes. Pick up on just one of these great new ideas, and it'll make your day.

**Simply Safer** tips help you do what is necessary to make your home safer and more secure. Whether it's shutting out burglars or checking to be sure that your fire extinguisher is up to snuff, any of these clever, easy-to-follow tips will help to keep your family members and guests safer around the house.

**Stress Busters** will help you lighten up while getting the job done. These uplifting tidbits help you focus on what needs doing to keep your home presentable—while ignoring the rest. If you think you really have to do it all, relax! It isn't so.

**Cost Cutters** offer tips for keeping your home stylish and functional without dipping into the kids' college fund. Here's vivid proof that with a little bit of creativity and smart shopping, your household can thrive on a modest budget.

**Rules of Thumb** make it easy to get a grip on the job of estimating quantities and coping with common household challenges. These are the guidelines many professionals use when determining how to handle repair and decorating jobs.

**Don't Forget** tips remind you that there are simpler ways to tackle just about everything on your household agenda. At first glance, ideas in this category may seem obvious—but they will save you effort in the long run, and they'll safeguard your household against expensive and frustrating mistakes.

# ORGANIZING
## your Home

—✳—

**1** **Take inventory** of your home's contents and note any problems with existing storage and display areas. **2** Free up space by getting **rid** of what you can. **3** Place items you decide to **keep** in the rooms where you'll use them, or where they most please you. **4** Identify unneeded items you can't bear to part with and **store** them away. **5** **Exploit unused space,** including areas beneath stairs, under beds, and over doors. **6** Install **space savers,** such as a shower caddy in the bath or shelves in the living room. **7** **Group** small decorative items or collections together on tabletops or shelves. **8** Consolidate or **stack** bigger items, such as the TV and VCR. Consider a wall storage unit or an entertainment center if stacking proves unfeasible. **9** When purchasing new furniture, choose pieces with **built-in storage,** such as beds with drawers beneath the mattress, wall storage units for home-office equipment, and coffee tables with cabinets or shelves underneath. **10** Set aside a little time each evening to return the day's **misplaced items** to their proper locations. ●

# Everything in Its Place

## MAKING SPACE FOR WHAT'S IMPORTANT

*——*——*

With homes becoming a center for both work and family life, we're keeping more inside them than ever before. It seems as if most homes aren't built with enough places to hold our growing piles of belongings. If you've ever sat down to pay bills at a cluttered desk or frantically searched for a suit in a bulging closet, you know how frustrating it can be to have too little space for the things you use.

But even if you could snap your fingers and make another closet appear, more space wouldn't be the answer. Without a system of organization, even the largest home would fill up over time. The logical solution is to get rid of what you don't need—and create storage space for what you do. By finding ways to keep clutter in check, you'll free up more time and space to enjoy the things you own. And you'll feel more confident inviting friends and family over to enjoy themselves in your newly spacious surroundings.

# Saying Good-bye to Clutter

Out of sight, out of mind, or so the adage goes. But you can go on dumping the excess of daily life into drawers, piling it in the basement, or tossing it in a box for only so long.

Sooner or later, the drawers will get stuck, the basement walkway will disappear, the box will overflow. And the already space-crunched surfaces in your home will be teeming with stuff. What's the solution? Begin by clearing out what you can, finding a place for what's left, and creating a system for organizing the new things that come through your doors.

The 19th-century English designer William Morris once said, "Have nothing in your houses that you do not know to be useful or believe to be beautiful." It is still sound advice, although it may seem hard-hearted: Who really wants to pitch the kids' favorite old toys or toss outdated but still comfortable clothes?

Although there's no need to throw out everything that fails to fit into Morris's two categories, you should still be selective. To decide what to keep and what to discard, ask yourself these questions:

◆ Have I used or enjoyed this item recently?

◆ Does someone in the family attach personal value to it?

◆ Would I save it if my house were burning down?

◆ Will I need it in the future?

If you've answered "no" to all of these questions, congratulate yourself. You've identified something you can eliminate in order to rid your home of clutter.

## WHERE TO START

Where should you begin? Wherever the results will have the most visible impact. If you normally enter your home through the living room, tackle that room first. If you come in through the garage, kitchen, or dining room, begin your job there.

Start by bringing five boxes or plastic lawn-and-leaf bags into the first room or entrance area. Fill one container with items that belong in other rooms, a second with items you can give away, a third with items to be stored, the fourth with the items you

## The In-and-Out Rule

Rules are made to be broken, but this dictum is one you won't want to violate: For each item you bring to your home, resolve to toss, recycle, or give away one item. It's the secret of a clutter-free household.

plan to toss out or recycle, and the fifth with all those things you want to include in your next garage sale.

Don't plan to make your first clutter-busting session a marathon. Instead, break down the job into small, manageable tasks. You're more likely to tackle a smaller job than you are to allot an entire Saturday to decluttering the whole house.

Go around the room or target area, starting from the highest point and working your way to the floor. Give each item you encounter—furniture, pictures on the wall, and items tucked in cabinets and drawers—careful consideration as to its usefulness or sentimental value to you and your family. If you can bear to live without the item, put it in the proper box or bag. Make a list of any large furnishings to be removed or relocated.

When your boxes or bags are brimming or you've given the area a thorough

## Reality Check

Rome wasn't built in a day, and your home doesn't have to be streamlined in such a short time, either. Think of organization as an ongoing process, a way of life. Try starting with small tasks whose results you'll appreciate every day—such as pruning out old medicines and cosmetics from the bathroom cabinet. You'll create a safer, more attractive space that will inspire you to continue your clutter-busting efforts.

**Airy and uncluttered,** *this room is spacious and free of extraneous furnishings. The secret is pieces that provide hidden storage, such as the chest that serves as a coffee table.*

**Show no mercy to the clutter that piles up in your home.**

once-over, return displaced items to their proper rooms. Make an appointment with your favorite charity to cart off the give-aways, or take the initiative and haul them away yourself. (Be sure to get a receipt for tax purposes.) Recycle or toss broken or unusable items. If you're going the garage-sale route, check your calendar for a good Saturday or Sunday in the weeks ahead and pencil in a specific date.

## Using Available Space

If you have stairs or high ceil-ings, you have potential storage space. Many stairways have small closets or storage areas underneath—the perfect place to stash the vacuum, mop, or other bulky items. If you have high ceilings, install a ledge way up along the wall to hold any of your bric-a-brac.

Transfer the items you'll be storing into sturdy filing boxes from an office-supply store or thick cardboard cartons from a moving company. Or take advantage of trunks or large suitcases that are sitting empty in your garage or attic. Make sure each container closes tightly to keep out dust, insects, and moisture, and label the containers so you won't have to open them later to know what's inside. For easier stacking, consider boxes of a similar size. Put the ones containing items you proba-bly won't need this year or next in the least accessible spots, and stow those boxes with items you may need in the months ahead in the most reachable places.

You can store some items temporarily in a rented storage unit near your home. After you complete the decluttering pro-cess, you'll be surprised at how much room you may have for them.

As your walls and floors begin to re-appear, take a good look around the room and consider how to organize the keepers. Items should take up residence where they are most convenient for you instead of where they are traditionally kept. Store batteries in the family room or the bedrooms where the kids' toys are, instead of in a kitchen drawer. Stash items that are normally used together—such as holiday decorations—in the same place rather than scattered in closets throughout your home. And why keep summer shorts and winter skiwear in the same box? You'll probably never use both at the same time.

Place things you use often in the most convenient spot. Put your frequently used pasta pots and saucepans in the front of the kitchen cupboard so you don't have to rifle through the pie plates or sauté pans to get to them. Store the videocassettes together on a waist-high living room shelf where they're easy to reach, instead of in an overhead cabinet or under the TV.

Obvious, yes, but as you discover more logical storage solutions, you may realize that you've been doing things the hard way until now. (For a summary of organizational steps, see the list on page 131.)

## SHOW IT OR HIDE IT

For those treasures that are meant to be seen, there are ways to display them attractively *and* compactly. For those you don't want on view, a clever hiding place is best.

Collections of small, decorative objects require a bit of togetherness to give them a bigger impact in the room—and to free up more precious space. Group items with a similar color, texture, shape, or theme together on tabletops or shelves rather than scattered about the room. Control tabletop turmoil by corralling the smallest items in interesting containers, baskets, or boxes, where they'll make a stronger statement.

## Emergency Clutter Holder

Strategically placing a basket, bin, or crate in your home's high-traffic areas—such as the kitchen or entryway—keeps mail, paperwork, and other small essentials from cluttering countertops and passageways. When you have a free moment, empty the hopper, returning each item to its proper place.

Make the most of your shelves—they're the ultimate weapons for combating clutter. If you don't have enough shelves, you can easily add a few more above dressers and consoles. They're terrific for organizing books, baskets, and bric-a-brac—those things you use occasionally or just can't bear to part with. Weigh the benefits of extra-high shelf space against the realization that you'll probably need a stepladder whenever you want to retrieve those items —and when you need to dust.

Are many of your possessions worth keeping but not worth looking at every day? If you're planning to add furnishings to your newly streamlined home, consider pieces that offer storage space. Next time you go shopping for living room furniture, look for coffee tables with drawers or cabinets underneath. Some chairs also have storage space. A bed with headboard storage or drawers beneath the mattress can save space in your bedroom.

## Screen Saver

No time or place to stash stuff?
For a quick temporary solution
to a storage problem, tuck the
vacuum cleaner, extra books,
linens—anything you don't know
what to do with—in a corner
and shield everything from sight
with an attractive folding screen.

If buying new furniture isn't an option, try to work with what you have. Skirt tables with fabric that falls to the floor to hide bulky items underneath. Or place these items in lidded baskets under your coffee table. Keep sweaters and blankets in plastic containers under your bed.

## BRING IN AN EXPERT

If you're too busy to organize your home yourself—or if you prefer to have someone else do it for you—hire a professional organizer. Part administrative assistant, part psychologist, part efficiency expert, and part mother, these professionals will listen to your clutter woes and design a system to alleviate them. To find a pro, ask a friend for references, call the National Association of Professional Organizers (see page 143), or search the Yellow Pages under "Organizing Services."

A good organizer will evaluate your home life, then create and install a system to help maximize your home's available space. He or she can supply a wealth of ideas and solutions—both "off the shelf" and customized—to help keep clutter from building up in the first place.

A professional will organize
you with military precision.

# ORDER IN THE HOUSE

---✦---

Now that you have made the necessary quick fixes, it's time to get down to some system-level retooling of your clutter hot spots. The big and little stuff in the living room. The busy kitchen.

The space-crunched bathroom. The cluttered kids' bedrooms. Your overburdened and much-used home office.

Even if you don't have time to go over every spot of your home—or can't seem to convince your little ones of the virtues of total tidiness—you can get more organized and help keep clutter in check. Here are some simple strategies to try.

**A streamlined kitchen** *makes for an inviting eating area. Built-in drawers free up precious counter space while storage bins on the shelves help keep items close but out of sight.*

## KITCHEN CLUTTER

The kitchen, by its nature, is probably the most heavily trafficked and most popular room in your home. It's where the family gets together during meals, friends gather during dinner parties, and you get each day off to a fresh start. A well-organized kitchen allows you to enjoy more fully every minute you spend in it.

Since the kitchen is where memories as well as meals are made, you'll need to consider both functionality and aesthetics as you organize each element inside. Does

# SIMPLE STORAGE IDEAS

✳

FOR A HOME THAT'S SIMPLY NEATER, create a special space for everything. First, look to items already available: Those miscellaneous mugs, wicker baskets, and extra coatracks can help corral the excesses of daily life—or showcase your prized possessions. Or try clearing clutter by placing it in sleek new storage containers.

**Tuck household bills** *out of sight—but not out of mind—inside a lidded rattan basket.*

**Showcase your fine** *millinery collection— or your children's prized baseball caps—on Shaker-style wall pegs or a simple coatrack.*

**Transparent plastic** *storage bins will neatly stack your wardrobe items in plain view.*

**Ceramic mugs, jelly jars,** *and small decorative flowerpots make great homes for pens, pencils, and other office supplies.*

**Hang garlic, onions,** *and herbs on wooden pegs (or use decorative hooks or even a small coatrack) to keep these staples easy to reach while you're cooking.*

your present setup work for you? Take this efficiency test: Make a list of your kitchen appliances—the blender, toaster, food processor, mixer—and note where each one is and how you use it. For instance, if your study shows that you're walking across the kitchen to carry bread to the toaster, then the toaster isn't housed in the most convenient place for you. Move it closer to the bread box or wherever you store bread. Do the same for other items whose locations you find to be inefficient.

## A PLACE FOR IT ALL

Organize drawers by grouping your most frequently used cooking tools in ceramic jars or other attractive holders on countertops. The drawers will be neater—with more space for other things—and you'll be able to get to these must-have utensils quicker. Clear canisters with airtight tops can hold and display such frequently used foodstuffs as bread, bagels, and pasta on countertops. When you can see a particular food item, you're more likely to eat it before it spoils. And you won't buy more of what you don't need.

Keep countertops uncluttered while using them for display. Place an attractive, shallow wicker basket, small wooden crate, or other container on a counter to hold treats for the kids or fill it with the snacks you like to grab on the run. Use antique, decorative tins or old-fashioned colored-glass mason jars to store your collections of tea bags and matchbooks—or as "hiding" places for dog biscuits and kitty treats.

Fruits and vegetables can take center stage in an attractive, breathable basket or

## Key Catchers

If your car and house keys go from hand to kitchen countertop each evening—only to get lost amid other items there—add a few hooks to a nearby wall to serve as key catchers. You'll cut down on countertop clutter and be able to locate your keys quickly on the way out the door each morning.

metal mesh container on the kitchen table or windowsill instead of taking up space —and being left to spoil unseen—in the back of the refrigerator. Let the fridge do double duty as a family message center: A magnetic message board on the doors will remind everyone in the family of the day's appointments and the week's schedule. The sides are a great place to display kids' artwork, family photos, take-out menus and a calendar for family activities. Who needs a desk in this busy place when a little creativity and a few magnets will do?

To keep telephone messages from becoming lost during the family's activities, keep a pad by the phone and secure a pen to it. If you have a space-saving telephone that mounts on the wall, be sure there's a writing surface and supplies nearby.

Inside drawers, use plastic sectional organizers or small oblong boxes to hold scissors, tape, and coupons in place—and to make them easier to find when you need them. These types of containers also work well for organizing large spoons, salad tongs, carving knives, corkscrews, and bottle and can openers.

If your cabinet shelves are not adjustable, subdivide the space with wire racks. It makes getting to pots, pans, dishes, and pie plates easier than when they're piled up all the way to the shelf above. This wire-rack system works equally well with items in the cupboards or pantry. You might also consider installing a corner cabinet carousel or rolling shelves.

You won't want to waste a single inch of precious cabinet space. Make the most of overhead cabinets by hanging stemmed glasses beneath them. Store your holiday cookware and the cake tins or roasting pans you use infrequently in those hard-to-reach cabinets high above the fridge.

**Look up for** *more kitchen storage. Hang pots and pans from a metal ceiling rack.*

Sort food—wherever you've stashed it—by category, to make things easy to reach. You'll also have a better idea of what needs restocking before you head out to the grocery store. Put baking items—such as flour, sugar, and baking soda and powder—in one area and cereals and canned fruits and vegetables in another. Alphabetize spices and put them on a shelf or rack mounted to the wall so you know what you have and can quickly grab what you need when you're cooking.

Instead of copying recipes from magazines or cookbooks onto file cards, create a recipe index in a small notebook. Jot down the names of your favorite recipes, the cookbook or magazine they are in, and the page number where you can find them. Place the index with your recipe books or magazines to make sure there will be no more frustrating searches when the last-minute dinner get-together is at your house. Keep recipes clipped from magazines in a file with folders labeled "Hors d'Oeuvres," "Main Dishes," and "Desserts."

Tame newspaper clutter by placing a small basket or bin in a pantry area to handle the day's discarded editions. Or make your own holder using a cardboard box. Simply cut slits down the center of each of the four sides of the box, place string through the openings and across the box; when the box is filled, tie the loose ends and remove the bundle for recycling.

Finally, to make everyday cleanups quicker, assign one large cabinet and one drawer near the dishwasher to serve as home for the daily dishes and silverware. If you have extra sets of dishes and far more place settings than you have household members, stock this area with just enough dishes and utensils to get everyone through the day and to make unloading the dishwasher less of a chore. Double the number of place settings if you run the dishwasher only every other day. Store the rest of the service in a place that's less

# UNCLUTTERING THE KITCHEN

✳

C OOKING UP SOLUTIONS FOR KITCHEN CLUTTER can be simpler
than you think. Just stock up on utility storage containers—
a countertop utensil jar, a tiered shelf maximizer, a bread box. Then
spice up the mix with decorative containers—humorous cookie jars,
quirky baskets—that add character even as they tame clutter.

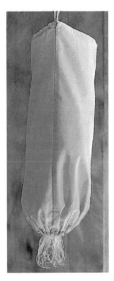

**Rustic wire baskets** *placed atop your kitchen counter showcase fresh fruits and vegetables or hold your family's favorite on-the-go snacks.*

**Modular storage units,** *inserted in a large cupboard, can double your space for napkins, place mats, and table linens. Or you can stock boxed pastas, canned fruits and vegetables, and cereals in the pullout drawers.*

**Hang a cloth** *cylinder with an opening at the bottom to store and dispense recycled plastic bags.*

**Designate a shallow** *basket in the kitchen or hallway as a holding center for mail.*

**Older bathrooms** *often lack built-in storage space. Hooks, pegs, and freestanding furniture can help reduce clutter there.*

convenient but still accessible, so it's handy when your meals require more dishes and glasses than you'd planned for.

## BRIGHTER BATHROOMS

The busy bathroom is the place to take advantage of the many tools and gadgets designed to organize your home's tight spaces. By design, most bathrooms leave little room for major improvement in terms of storage. Still, there are plenty of little things you can do to make the most of these cramped quarters.

Start the process by cleaning out the one major area in the bathroom that was designed specifically for toiletry storage— the medicine cabinet. Get rid of expired medications as well as any toiletries you've had for longer than two years, including shampoos, lotions and makeup, and soap. Besides creating more space, clearing out your cabinet will minimize health risks, as bacteria and fungi can contaminate lotions and cosmetics over time.

If you've cleaned everything possible out of your cabinet and you still can't control the clutter, consider installing a second wall-mounted medicine cabinet. Or you can hang a shower caddy over the shower-head to keep shampoo, shaving cream, soap, and razors within easy reach but somewhat out of eyesight.

Another space-maximizing device is a system of coated-wire rollout baskets, which can be used to expand the storage capacity of under-the-sink cabinet space. If your bathroom has no storage space there, mount a small coated-wire grid on the wall and hang personal appliances such as hair dryers and curling irons from it with S-hooks. You'll find these grids and rollout baskets at retailers that sell bath, kitchen, or closet storage accessories.

Take advantage of the empty space above the toilet by adding a small cabinet or shelves to hold extra linens or toiletries. Freestanding over-the-commode shelves can maximize this space right up to the ceiling. But be careful what you display here; small items that fall into the bowl will be no fun to retrieve.

You can also place your deodorant, perfume, hair dryer, and hairbrushes in the clear plastic pockets of a back-of-the-door shoe holder; this will keep these frequently used items from taking up counter space but within easy reach.

A second shower curtain rod, added behind and level with the first, provides a handy place to hang wet towels so they can air-dry before you fold and return them to the rack. If your shower has glass doors instead of a curtain and there's no place to hang a second rod, you can make more space for towels by replacing existing racks with sets of decorative hooks.

Since running out of toilet paper is something you'd like to avoid, store at least one spare roll in the bathroom rather than in the linen closet. Hide the extra roll in a simple covered basket with the lid slightly ajar. It remains discreetly hidden, yet you, your family, or a guest can grab it in a moment of need.

## LIVABLE LIVING ROOMS

The living room is home to some of the biggest, bulkiest objects you own. A couch and chairs. A coffee table. A television. The videocassette player and stereo equipment. Bookcases, end tables, and side tables. Perhaps even your home office and computer. And then there are the smaller treasures: favorite collections, coffee-table books, artwork, treasured mementos, photographs and photo albums, decorative lamps, vases, dried flowers, and candleholders.

## Mirror, Mirror

If you can't squeeze another bit of space out of your bathroom, create the illusion of roominess instead. A large mirror on the wall (opposite the window, if you have one) can make even the tiniest of powder rooms seem larger and brighter because it will reflect both the natural and artificial light.

Start retooling this family hub by taking a good look around the room. Are your shelves too jam-packed to do justice to the photos, book collections, and family heirlooms that vie for space there? If so, begin by stripping the shelves bare of all objects. After a good dusting, put things back in a balanced assortment of large and small items. Place books you rarely read on the

**Making order out of apparent chaos can involve little more than moving a few things around or adding a shelf or two.**

With so many different objects competing for space, a living room can start looking like a crowded curio shop. But making order out of apparent chaos isn't as hard as it seems. It can involve little more than moving a few things around, adding a shelf or two, perhaps investing in an inexpensive wall storage system—and, above all, using what you have. The main goal here is to create a room in which family members and guests feel comfortable.

shelf nearest the floor and a grouping of smaller, lighter items on the next shelf up. Display items you'd like at center stage on chest-high shelves, and place the remaining items higher up, alternating between bulky pieces and delicate objects.

Look high and low for the objects that have strayed from other rooms and been haphazardly set atop the television, coffee table, or end tables. Return them to their rightful homes, or move them into storage.

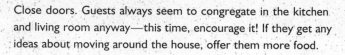

## SIMPLE SOLUTIONS

# EMERGENCY DECLUTTERING

THE HOUSE LOOKS, WELL, LIVED-IN, and your friends are on their way over for a visit. There's no time for the thorough cleaning your house needs. So try these quick fixes instead:

**Simple**

Gather up the most obvious clutter—newspapers, magazines, toys, and stray shoes—and deposit it in a bedroom or out-of-the-way den until the end of the evening.

**Simpler**

In areas adjacent to the living room, move the reminders of daily life against a wall to the right or left of the door, where they'll be out of your guests' immediate line of sight.

**Simplest**

Close doors. Guests always seem to congregate in the kitchen and living room anyway—this time, encourage it! If they get any ideas about moving around the house, offer them more food.

---

Next, if your couch, chairs, and other furnishings are flush against the wall, move them to the center of the room in seating clusters, or as a single grouping with items spaced 8 to 10 feet (2–3m) apart. This will create a more intimate seating area and, more important, it will free up a wall for new shelves or cabinets.

Use the additional shelves to relieve clutter on existing shelves or to display some bigger items that have been visually

**Wall storage units can be a godsend. They can hide office equipment or even foldout beds for guests.**

lost elsewhere in the room. The ceiling is the limit. Or consider placing a decorative table or small cabinet behind the sofa and using it to show off large framed pictures or other bulky items.

While you wouldn't want to cover every wall in your living room with shelves, more wall space does mean more storage possibilities. Consider the walls a display gallery for your treasured items. Hang antique fireplace tools near the hearth, your flute from grade school amid a collection of music-inspired prints, or a child's framed drawing among family photos.

## HIDING IT AWAY

Wall storage units can be a godsend. Consider hiding home-office equipment inside an attractive storage unit instead of keeping it exposed on a four-legged table. Some systems come with folding work tables and deep file drawers. A few even include a foldout bed for overnight guests.

Other large-scale storage possibilities include antique or wicker trunks, wooden storage chests, and benches with hinged seats and hollow compartments.

Store the small stuff in Shaker-style boxes, decorative bowls, colorful cookie jars, and wicker baskets. Consider a CD album for your discs; a media tower—an upright stacker for your videocassettes; and a cord and cable organizer that encloses in one cablelike conduit all those unsightly wires behind the TV and stereo.

## CLEARING CLOSETS

Does it take more than a minute to locate a favorite outfit in your closet? Do your freshly laundered or dry-cleaned clothes come off the hanger in need of pressing? Do you wear the same clothes each week, even though you pride yourself on your updated wardrobe? If you answered "yes" to any of these questions, you could save time and rejuvenate your wardrobe by streamlining your closet.

Start by removing all the clothes and accessories from your closet and organizing them by type: shirts, pants, suits, dresses, coats, shoes, belts, and handbags. Set aside the things you don't wear anymore, and consider their future. Here are a few possibilities for dealing with these items:

◆ STORE WINTER OR SUMMER GARMENTS UNTIL THE APPROPRIATE SEASON.

◆ UPDATE OLD CLOTHES BY HAVING THEM ALTERED.

◆ DONATE UNWANTED WARDROBE ITEMS TO CHARITY.

◆ SELL EXPENSIVE ARTICLES ON CONSIGNMENT.

◆ USE SOFT, WORN-OUT CLOTHES AS CLEANING OR CAR-WASHING RAGS.

Among the remaining garments, you'll probably find numerous wrinkled but

## Space for Clothes

How much room will you need for clothes? Professional closet organizers generally allot one linear foot (30cm) of hanging space for 6 suits, 8 dresses, 12 shirts, or 6 pairs of pants.

wearable items that you haven't slipped on recently because you couldn't find them. Make a mental note to place these "aha!" items in plain view.

Now is a good time to evaluate your past storage methods and consider how you can be more efficient. Have you spent far too much time searching for the right shirt to go with your favorite suit? Consider hanging the two pieces side by side. Are you a separates mix-and-matcher? Then group separates by color (so you can quickly scan for the day's color scheme) or by type of garment, placing blazers next to shirts and pants beside skirts. Decide whether it would be easier for you to view your clothes by type (work clothes and weekend wear), outfit, color, or length, and then arrange your closet accordingly.

You can double your space by adding a second rod below shorter items such as shirts and folded-over trousers. Then hang more of the same there. Alternatively, you might consider adding shelves for your T-shirts, sweaters, and shoes beneath hanging items. After all, when your clothing is buried inside dresser drawers, it's out of sight and less likely to be worn. What's more, hanging a knitted or lightweight garment on a hanger can distort the shape of the fabric, detracting from its appearance and requiring more frequent—and time-consuming—pressing.

What about those odds and ends that can clutter drawers and dresser tops? Hang a mesh laundry bag in your closet to keep socks, stockings, handkerchiefs, and other small items easy to find. Try looping belts over a hanger next to your pants, or hang them on hooks inside the door. You can store hats or bags this way as well.

If rearranging your closet's contents still leaves you with more stuff than room, it's time to bring in reinforcements. There are plenty of inexpensive organizing tools that can help you maximize your wardrobe space. Back-of-the-door shoe bags keep shoes off the floor and in plain sight. Also, there are plenty of racks for scarves, ties, belts, hats, and other accessories that can save space in your closet.

If the basic design of your closet simply isn't functional for your wardrobe or leaves you short a hanging rod or three, you have several simple options: You can buy a new or antique freestanding armoire or wardrobe. You can purchase a prefabricated closet kit (available at stores that specialize in home organization or from several catalogs) and retool the space yourself. Or you can hire a closet designer to create a system (see the Yellow Pages under "Closets and Closet Accessories").

## TAMING KIDS' CLUTTER

If the patter of little feet is a familiar sound in your home, then the sight of pint-size clutter probably is, too. Rainbow drawings, aced tests, and miscellaneous school papers arrive home daily with the kids. And afternoons are an adventurous whirl of crayons, paints, books, and toys.

Messiness is a normal part of childhood. Most kids grow into neat—or at least neater—adults. But that doesn't mean you have to give in to clutter until your kids head off to college. Gather the kids together and set some ground rules: Toys

Taming clutter and organizing
your closet can require discipline.

mustn't block doorways. Clean clothes, tried on and rejected, must go back to the drawer instead of into the dirty-clothes hamper. Everything must be picked up and put away by bedtime.

Once you have these rules in place, look around your home for furnishings that can be recycled to the kids' rooms. Instill an appreciation of your family's past by turning items with sentimental value into unique storage spots for their precious treasures. Turn a trunk or footlocker into a storage compartment for athletic gear or toys. As a precaution, disengage the lock and add a safety latch or other device that keeps the lid securely open.

Use a small dresser to store the kids' artwork in the family room or a child's bedroom. Store art supplies atop a dresser in tin beach pails; add a basket to hold fresh paper. Let the kids fill the drawers with their daily creations. You can't save every crayon drawing or finger painting, so pick the best effort of each week, or weed out the drawers when they are full and stash the treasures away in a special box with the child's name on it. You can also include school photos, notes from the teacher, and other special papers.

Let a mug rack—hung low—serve as a hitching post for the kids' miscellaneous possessions, such as belts, hats, necklaces, and gloves. In the bath, a laundry lingerie bag or a corner organizer with holes that allow water to drain out will keep those rubber ducks, sailboats, and Barbies from taking over the tub.

Finally, place a bin or a sturdy basket in each of the main rooms where your

KEEPING KIDS' CLUTTER IN CHECK IS CHILD'S PLAY WHEN YOU HAVE PLACES TO STASH GAMES AND TOYS.

### Stackable bins

Open-front bins will keep toys off the floor where they might cause someone to trip, yet let kids retrieve playthings without assistance. Stackable units are a blessing if your child has more toys than one bin can hold.

### Transparent lidded boxes

Stow toys that don't get daily use in a large plastic box. Because kids can always keep an eye on the contents, they probably won't protest. Stash boxes of second-string toys in the back of a closet or under a bed.

### Toy chest

Consider an attractive toy chest to house frequently used toys. It can also be a sturdy seat for parents to sit on while helping kids get dressed in the morning. But make sure the chest has a lightweight or removable lid that won't slam down and hurt a child.

### Small baskets

Shallow wicker baskets—the kind adults use to sort mail—are equally efficient for storing toy soldiers, action figures, and stray dinosaurs. For added kid appeal, purchase baskets in bright, eye-popping colors.

children play. Teach your kids to deposit their toys there when they move from one room to the next. Your nighttime cleanup ritual will be quicker and simpler, as the kids will need to go to only one place in each room to retrieve the toys they've played with during the day.

If you're in the market for a good-size stuff-holder, steer clear of the uncovered

lets you organize the paper flow is crucial to staying on top of your personal and professional responsibilities.

Keeping good records not only helps you find key documents quickly, it also saves time and eliminates headaches. And with everything neatly filed away or in its rightful place, your work area suddenly seems a model of efficiency.

**If your desk is a table, a lidded box that can be shut tight
will protect your paperwork from kids and pets.**

toy boxes you'll come across in many stores —they just collect dust in addition to an unsightly jumble of toys and books that eventually spills onto the floor. Choose clear plastic boxes with snap-on lids—they allow your children to see what's inside. They also make great space maximizers, since most are stackable.

## THE PAPER CHASE

Whether your home office has a room of its own or is confined to the dining room or a nook in your bedroom, a system that

## Priority Mail

To keep paper pileups to a minimum, make opening mail your first priority. If you respond to everything as soon as it comes in, you'll feel up-to-date—even if it's the only thing you tackle in your home office that day.

For starters, your home office will need a few business basics. These include an easy-to-use filing system (a file drawer or cabinet with hanging files, manila file folders with plenty of stick-on tab labels), a trash can and a recycling bin or box, a letter opener, stamps, and places to stack incoming and outgoing mail. Make sure the chair beneath your work surface is supportive and at a comfortable height, especially if you use a computer. If the chair is comfortable, you're more likely to sit there longer and get more done without hand or eye strain.

Next, make sure that whatever space you've chosen is safe from curious little fingers, the dog's teeth, or the cat's claws. If you have a separate office, a closed door should keep all the little ones out. If your desk is a table in a corner, a lidded box that can be shut tight will protect your paperwork at night. Or consider file drawers or a hanging file basket with a lid.

Organize your papers into categories that make sense to you. These can include tax information (canceled checks, receipts,

Keep pets away from papers—your dog may use a different filing system than you do.

pay stubs), items that need response (invitations or requests for information), items to save (coupons, appliance instructions, warranties), phone and mailing lists, and correspondence. Place these sorted papers into files that you have set up.

You may also want to create an "in" box for those items that have arrived with the daily mail that you don't have time to read or file. If you're crunched for time, tuck "to reads" in the back of your daily planner and pull them out when you're standing in the grocery line or waiting to pick up the kids at school.

If you bring work home from your office, you'll want to create a separate area, drawer, hanging desktop file, or group of folders in your home for organizing professional papers and journals.

If you're in the habit of taking notes on scraps of paper—only to have them disappear, more often than not, without a trace—resolve to write notes only in an appropriate place, such as in the right file or your appointment book, or on full-size sheets of paper that are harder to misplace.

Set aside 10 to 15 minutes each day (it's easy to remember if it's the first thing you do) to go through mail and get rid of what you can from your in box. If you find that you're tossing or recycling the same things each week, consider stopping subscriptions to magazines you don't have time to read and writing to an appropriate organization to halt unwanted junk mail (see page 143).

## Desktop Hot Spot

Create a "hot spot" on your desktop for correspondence, bills, and other items that require your immediate attention. Use a basket, wire box, or desktop hanging file that's convenient for you and stashed where the kids can't get to it. Budget 10 minutes each morning or each evening to go through the pile and tackle the single most pressing item inside.

# HOW to KEEP HOUSEWORK
# from RULING Your Life

——✳——

**1** If it isn't **begging** for attention, don't clean it. If dirt and dust aren't obvious, leave them for later. **2** Make the most of every minute. Find **tasks** that you can do simultaneously. **3** Head off housework. Use a **doormat** to keep dirt outside; eat only in the kitchen or dining room. **4** Avoid interruptions. Allow the **answering machine** to take calls until you've finished the task at hand. **5** Set realistic cleaning **standards.** If you lack the time to clean your home thoroughly, adjust your expectations. **6** Call in the troops. A family that **works together** has more time to play together. **7** Keep household germs **in check.** Make time for bathroom and kitchen disinfecting. **8** Say adieu to allergens. **Vacuum** frequently and wash bed linens in hot water to remove dust mites. **9** Thin your **houseplant** collection. If you enjoy indoor greenery but hate taking care of it, choose a few easy-care plants and weed out the rest. **10** Make your **home safe.** A clutter-free home helps prevent accidents from happening. ●

# REDEFINING HOUSEWORK

## FREEING YOURSELF
## FROM HOUSEHOLD DRUDGERY

\* —— \* —— \*

These days, between family commitments and workplace obligations, parents are busier than ever. It's hard enough to get home by 6 P.M., let alone sift through the day's mail, prepare the family's evening meal, and manage to squeeze in a little daily housecleaning. How can you find time to do the necessary chores—and still have a life?

Relax. You can get the essential cleaning tasks done each week, and still have time to savor your weekends. Part of the secret lies in breaking down big household jobs into smaller, more manageable tasks. The rest of the secret lies in enlisting everyone in the family to help get it all done.

Add to this mix the simple fact that there are many more efficient cleaning products and energy-saving tools available to you, and you'll find that it's possible to have a clean, safe home *and* time to enjoy it with family and friends.

# CLEANING STRATEGIES FOR BUSY BODIES

---✳---

Htriangle OW CAN YOU MANAGE THE CHALLENGE OF GETTING THE KIDS OFF TO SCHOOL, WORKING A FULL-TIME JOB, COOKING DINNER, AND SQUEEZING IN A FEW ESSENTIAL HOUSEKEEPING CHORES IN YOUR SPARE TIME?

Start by rethinking your definition of *clean*. Sure, Mom may have vacuumed and polished every day, but you don't have to. While there are chores you won't want to skip, some niceties can be dispensed with now and then. For example, if the carpet doesn't look dirty, don't vacuum it. If dust bunnies aren't crowding the wood floors, save sweeping for another time.

Yes, you'll have to do these chores eventually, and if guests are coming you'll want to make things presentable straightaway. But for day-to-day living, don't sweat the small stuff.

In order to get the freedom to truly enjoy your leisure time, do your cleaning in spurts during the week instead of all on the weekend. Break down big jobs, such as cleaning the bathroom, into smaller tasks: Wipe down the sink now; clean the bathtub and mop the floor later. When it is time to tackle the room's other surfaces, you'll be ahead of the cleaning game.

Any job seems overwhelming if you can't compartmentalize it—and cleaning the house is no exception. But you can maintain your home *and* your composure.

## PREVENTIVE ACTION

When it comes to keeping your home tidy, a little preventive action goes a long way. Stop dirt at the door by having people remove their shoes before entering. Or invest in a good doormat. Indoors, place washable rugs in high-traffic areas to prevent dirt from being tracked from room to room. Confine eating to the kitchen or dining room so you won't be chasing crumbs in the rest of the house.

Head off clutter. Few people will ever notice dust on top of the refrigerator, but

## Don't Worry, Be Happy

Your sanity and your family's serenity are far more important than a sparkling-clean home will ever be. If you're crunched for time, skip the dusting and the vacuuming this week and just do laundry and dish duty. A bare-bones cleaning now will keep your home running smoothly and help keep stress in check. Besides, it's highly unlikely a white-gloved drill sergeant will come knocking on your front door anytime soon.

they'll immediately register items that are strewn around the living room. If you have only a minute, opt for put-away duty in lieu of a cleaning task.

Return everything to its proper place the minute you've finished using it, rather than waiting until the end of the day, by which time the pickup job will likely be overwhelming. Tackle the small jobs before they turn into big ones: Sweep up crumbs before they get ground into kitchen floors or family room carpeting.

And when you finally snatch a magic cleaning moment, make sure you don't get sidetracked. If you're only partway through organizing the refrigerator shelves, let the answering machine take that call. If you're shopping online for a new kitchen mixer and Aunt Agnes sends an e-mail, add her communiqué to the others to be answered when your transaction is complete.

*When you confine* eating to the kitchen and dining areas, you prevent the inevitable tracking of crumbs into the rest of the home.

Finally, having the troops pitch in is an important part of getting it all done in the allotted time. Give every member of your family a cleaning task to accomplish. And if the results aren't perfect, well, that's just the way things are. Let them be.

## SIMPLE SOLUTIONS

# AVOIDING DISTRACTIONS

LIFE BY ITS VERY NATURE is a series of distractions. But that's no excuse for getting sidetracked. There is much you can do to curtail the number of interruptions. Here are a few strategies to help you stay focused and get it all done.

**Simple**

Request quiet time. Block off a specific time of day when you can work alone. Tell family members that you're not to be disturbed and that you'll let them know when you're through.

**Simpler**

Sequester yourself. Shut the door to your home office or bedroom until the task is completed. Take the phone off the hook or let the answering machine handle any calls.

**Simplest**

Plan ahead. Take advantage of those times when the house is the quietest. Work on projects when the kids are at school or before your mate arrives home from work.

# DOUBLE DUTY

---✳---

TOO MUCH TO DO AND NOT ENOUGH TIME TO DO IT? Chances are you can add a simple housekeeping task to whatever you're doing at home so that every moment does double duty. Here are a few ideas.

**While...**

**microwaving dinner.** Wipe down kitchen walls and baseboards; manage microwave spills while waiting for your piping-hot meal to cool off a bit—spills are a snap to wipe up before they settle and harden.

**making coffee.** Declutter your countertops; organize the kitchen shelves that house cups and glasses; sweep out stray crumbs from the food cabinet; scrub the kitchen sink clean of a day's worth of dirt.

**opening mail.** Station yourself near a trash can or recycling bin where you can toss junk mail and envelopes; sort bills on the spot and file them for payment later.

**cooking.** Wash utensils and dishes and put them away as you go; wipe down cooktop spills as soon as they happen; arrange pots and pans for easy access; straighten up the spice rack.

**taking out the trash.** Organize the recycling bin—glass, metal, and paper; brush away leaves and debris from the trash-storage area; pick up litter from the curb; check on outdoor plants and make a mental note of gardening to-dos.

**waiting out TV commercials.** Dash into the kitchen—but not for a handful of potato chips. This is the perfect time to wipe the remnants of dinner from the countertops, finish loading the dishwasher, organize the utility drawer, or do a quick sweeping of the kitchen floor.

**waiting in the doctor's office.** Pay bills and balance your checkbook; jot a quick postcard to a friend you haven't heard from in a while; address Christmas-card envelopes; review your calendar and respond to invitations.

**waiting for the kettle to boil.** Check your e-mail and write replies; visit your favorite Web sites; feed the dog or cat; change the cat's litter box; water your plants and police flower pots for dead leaves or blossoms.

**waiting for the kids to get dressed.** Put away the breakfast dishes, wash the coffeepot, empty the trash, warm up the car.

**talking on the phone.** Organize the linen closet; fold and sort clothes; unload the dishwasher; dust the living room and dining room; water and groom houseplants.

**putting away groceries.** Check the refrigerator for any leftovers that have been hanging around too long and toss them; arrange food in like categories; wipe down the refrigerator doors and clean out the vegetable bins; rotate older pantry items to the front.

**allowing the oven cleaner to work.** Clean the grime from the windowsills; clip coupons; declutter the kitchen table; weed through stacks of old newspapers, catalogs, and magazines and toss discards into the recycling bin.

**waiting for repair people.** Sweep and mop the kitchen floor; straighten up all the books, pictures, and various knickknacks displayed on shelves; dust all surfaces in the living room, dining room, and hallway; organize cluttered kitchen cabinets; polish the mirrors.

**taking a shower.** Sprinkle cleanser on the tub or shower floor and push a sponge around with your foot while you're waiting for your conditioner to soak in; while soaking in the tub use an old toothbrush to scrub tile grout.

# THE ART OF DELEGATION

———— ✳ ————

IF YOU'VE ALREADY MANAGED TO GET OTHER FAMILY MEMBERS ON THE JOB, BRAVO. BUT IF YOU'VE FOUND THAT YOU'RE CONSTANTLY DOING ALL THE WORK YOURSELF, THEN THE TIME HAS COME TO PASS THE MOP.

Sharing the load is as important for others as it is for you. If you constantly pick up after your children, they won't learn the basic cleaning skills they'll need as adults. What's more, an uneven workload will often cause tension between spouses or between the children and the grown-up members of the household.

While the time you spend initially in cajoling extra helpers and showing them the ropes may seem like more trouble than it's worth, you'll soon find that delegating has its benefits. You'll not only buy yourself free time, you'll also eliminate the nagging resentment you may feel toward other family members who aren't pulling their weight. Your children will benefit by learning responsibility—which will make them good little guests who are sure to be invited back to friends' homes.

With kids, you'll need to set a couple of ground rules: One, no fun stuff until all of their chores are done; and two, any chores that come up at the last minute must be completed upon request. This rule is one you may need to invoke when friends from around the corner call to say that they'll be dropping by and you need the house primed—fast.

With your spouse, the compromise approach will probably work best. Divide the work fairly. Each of you takes the jobs you like best (or dislike least), then you apportion the remaining chores equally.

When to clean? If weekends around your house are when the troops gather, that's the perfect time to rally them. Give each person a list of chores and allow an hour for everyone to complete the tasks. If, however, weekends are on-the-go times

You didn't mess up the house alone, so why not get everyone to help clean it?

**Older teens can** *handle chores that demand more responsibility. This lightens your load and gives them a greater sense of importance.*

for the family, post a chart on the refrigerator that lists each person's chores for the morning, after school, and evening.

## HOW KIDS CAN HELP

Granted, getting kids to help with cleaning isn't easy. Besides, how much help can you realistically expect from a child? The answer depends on your child's age:

*Ages 3 to 4.* Encourage preschoolers to put away playthings after use. They can also put dirty clothing in the hamper, keep their rooms neat, and wipe their feet before coming inside. With supervision, they can remove unbreakable and blunt-edged items from the dishwasher, dust low furniture, and water plants. By making cleanup the precursor to a fun activity, and by helping until your child masters the tasks, you can make cleaning an enjoyable, confidence-building activity.

*Ages 5 to 9.* Grade-school kids can wipe up spills, secure the tops on plastic

containers of leftovers, make their beds, take care of pets, set and clear the table, fold laundry items, unpack groceries, and help with simple cooking tasks like washing vegetables and spreading pizza sauce.

*Ages 10 to 13.* Preteens and younger teenagers can clean up after most art projects, prepare their own lunches and wipe countertops afterward, clean their rooms, load and unload the dishwasher or wash and dry the dishes, dust, and vacuum.

*Ages 14 to 17.* Older teens can tackle bigger jobs, such as cleaning the kitchen or bathroom or washing clothes. Kids at this stage are really learning life skills.

Adding such responsibilities to your child's daily routine lightens the workload for everyone and gives you all more time to spend together. Best of all, it instills a stronger sense of your family as a team.

## Motivating Kids

Resist the urge to reward your children for their housekeeping help—compensation tells kids a task is above and beyond the call of duty. Instead, let younger children know specifically what chores you expect them to do, and let the satisfaction of a job well done provide its own reward. Let teenagers know they are contributing more to the family and learning skills that will help them in life.

# KEEPING YOUR HOME HEALTHY

---　✳　---

HOME MAY BE WHERE THE HEART IS, BUT IT IS ALSO WHERE GERMS, DUST, MOLD AND MILDEW, AND OTHER ALLERGENS SET UP SHOP. THESE NASTY, INVISIBLE INTERLOPERS THRIVE EVEN IN HOUSEHOLDS THAT LOOK CLEAN.

They ride home from school on your child's hands, hitch rides on your purse or briefcase, enter with foods that you bring home, and grow and multiply beneath the sink. If left unchecked, they can cause all kinds of illnesses, ranging from the common cold and allergy attacks to food poisoning and hepatitis A.

Although you really can't hope to eliminate such irritants entirely, there are some simple housekeeping tasks that will help you to keep these menacing germs and allergens at bay. By focusing your cleaning efforts on the major germ and allergy hot spots, you'll be able to keep things well under control.

## WHERE GERMS LURK

Light switches, telephones, computer keyboards, remote controls for the VCR and TV, and doorknobs, are favorite spots for any of the 150 sneeze- and cough-creating common cold viruses today. Such places are also favored by the lesser-known but equally unpleasant rotavirus, which causes diarrhea, especially in infants. These bugs

Arm yourself with disinfectant, and then shoot to kill.

# LIVING WITH PETS
# YOU'RE ALLERGIC TO

ANIMALS ARE WELL-LOVED FAMILY MEMBERS. Despite the fact that they sometimes make us cough and sneeze, we still want them around. Below are tips to help you cope.

**Simple**

Dust carefully, being sure to hit every nook and cranny. Sweep up pet hair, and vacuum regularly. Even if you don't see any pet hair, you can assume that it's everywhere.

**Simpler**

Wash Fido or Fluffy once a week in a tub filled with lukewarm water. If that's too much to handle on your own, take your four-legged friend to a groomer for a professional scrub-down.

**Simplest**

As much as you'd like to invite that cute bundle of fur to sleep with you, don't do it. In fact, close your bedroom door and make that space off-limits to canines and felines.

can survive for hours on hard surfaces in the home, especially plastics and metals, as well as on children's toys.

If someone in your family has all the telltale signs of a cold virus or complains of intestinal upset, clean and disinfect the common surfaces and toys in your home daily until symptoms disappear. A cleaner labeled "disinfectant" will kill most tough germs on hard surfaces. Spray directly on an area, and let the solution do its work for 10 minutes. Wipe dry with a paper towel or lint-free cloth. As a preventive measure, disinfect these surfaces weekly.

Areas prone to dampness—such as bathroom surfaces; the washing machine, humidifier, and air conditioner; and the area under kitchen, bathroom, and laundry room sinks—provide perfect breeding grounds for mold and mildew, which are major causes of allergies. Keep any water

mopped up in these spots and clean away surface mold with a fungicide or a bleach-and-water solution. You might wear a dust mask to protect your lungs from any mold spores stirred up while cleaning.

Show airborne germs and allergens an exit by regularly opening the windows in your home. Ventilation allows germs to dissipate. By diminishing humidity, it also discourages mold growth.

## SNIFFLE-FREE SLEEP

Your cozy bed is a snug spot for dust and dust mites to settle in. These allergy triggers thrive in sheets, blankets, pillows, carpets and rugs, and on drapes and blinds. While they are impossible to obliterate, they're actually harmless unless you have allergies. Still, you may rest more comfortably if you take a few steps to keep these microscopic culprits in check.

Wash your bed linens once a week in the hottest water safe for your sheets. Your comforter, blanket, and pillows should be washed at least monthly. Damp-wipe or vacuum your blinds regularly—they're a virtual magnet for dust.

If you have feather pillows or a goose-down comforter and you often sneeze all through the night, try changing to polyester bedding (it doesn't attract dust mites as much as cotton and feathers do) or consider encasing all of your bedding—both mattress and box springs—in a nonallergenic plastic cover. This item is available from allergy supply companies.

**The most effective weapon in the war against allergens is a vacuum cleaner with a special HEPA (high-efficiency particle absorbent) filter. It's expensive, but worth it.**

Regularly vacuuming—at least weekly—can help keep your home's allergen count down to livable levels. At grocery stores or through companies that supply antiallergy products, you can purchase dust-filtering vacuum bags, an inexpensive way to keep most of the sucked-up dust from escaping through the exhaust. The most effective weapon in the war against allergens is a vacuum cleaner with a special HEPA (high-efficiency particle absorbent) filter. This type of vacuum cleaner is expensive, but worth the price for those troubled by severe allergies. Or you can upgrade your existing vacuum with an ultrafine filter designed to trap tiny dust particles. You'll generally find these filters through allergy supply companies, though many grocery stores are beginning to stock them alongside traditional vacuum filters.

As a preventive measure, allergy sufferers should consider eliminating major dust catchers in bedrooms, such as stuffed animals and carpeting or large rugs. If you can't remove these, be sure to vacuum the area often, especially under beds.

## BATHROOM BASICS

Microscopic life thrives in all bathrooms. Without the proper strategies in place, even your toothbrush isn't safe from cold viruses, rotavirus, salmonella, *Escherichia coli* bacteria, and mold and mildew. These pathogens and allergens flourish in and on toilets, on faucets, on the floor and walls, and in damp towels and washcloths.

**A bathroom can** *look clean but still be brimming with microscopic life. A weekly disinfecting will help keep germs in check.*

Make it a weekly priority to disinfect the toilet, sink, and faucet handles, using a disinfectant cleaner or diluted bleach and water. Apply the cleaner, let it stand on the surface for 10 minutes, and wipe clean with a paper towel or lint-free cloth. Regularly clean the base of your soap dish in the shower and on the sink. Every three days or so, replace used bath towels and washcloths with clean ones.

Your best defense against all disease-causing organisms is always to wash your hands with soap and warm water after using the toilet. Teach your children this important safety rule early. Close the lid of the toilet before you flush to prevent stirred-up germs from escaping into the air and settling on bathroom surfaces.

After using towels, fold or hang them loosely to dry; this helps prevent germs and mold from getting a toehold. Use a toothbrush cover to prevent airborne germs,

yeast, and molds from colonizing on the bristles and getting into your mouth; or consider a toothbrush sanitizer. This item is available from allergy supply companies.

## KITCHEN CULPRITS

In the kitchen, proper handling of raw meat, fish, and poultry can stop most germs associated with them from multiplying to levels that can make you and your family ill. While most pathogens that occur naturally in uncooked foods are killed by proper cooking—to an internal temperature of at least 145°F (63°C) for roasts or chops of beef, veal, or lamb; 160°F (72°C) for ground meats; and 180°F (83°C) for poultry—many germs can spread long before you pop the entrée into the oven. *E. coli,* hepatitis A, and salmonella—the most common contaminants—can find their way onto a sponge or dishcloth; you, in turn, can then spread the bacteria all over your kitchen unless you make an effort to stop them.

The single most important thing you can do to ensure your family's health and safety is to wash your hands with warm, soapy water for at least 20 seconds before and after preparing food. This will prevent you from spreading meat-, poultry-, or fish-borne bacteria onto refrigerator doors, cabinet handles, and countertops, where they'll be lying in wait next time you reach for a leftover slice of pizza.

In addition to washing your hands, you can help prevent cross-contamination by washing in hot, soapy water the utensils used to prepare your raw food. That includes all knives, cutting boards, and

## Drain Duty

Those leftover food particles in your moist drain and disposal unit create an ideal environment for bacterial growth. You should sanitize the drain, disposal, and connecting pipe periodically by pouring in a solution of 1 teaspoon (5ml) chlorine bleach in 1 quart (1L) of water, or use a commercial kitchen disinfectant according to product directions.

# How Long Foods Last

---- ✳ ----

YOU KNOW WHEN THE LETTUCE IN YOUR FRIDGE has turned: It's more brown than green. But what about other foods you store at home? Check expiration dates, and follow these guidelines.

| PANTRY ITEMS | Unopened (on shelf) | Opened (in fridge) |
|---|---|---|
| Condiments | 2 months to 1 year | 1 to 6 months |
| Flour, all-purpose | 6 to 8 months | |
| Fruit, canned | 2 years | 1 week* |
| Jams, jellies, preserves | 1 year | 6 months |
| Pasta, dried | 2 years | |
| Peas, canned | 3 years | 2 to 4 days* |
| Rice, white or wild | 18 months to 2 years | 1 year (uncooked) |
| Soda and carbonated water | 3 to 9 months | 2 to 3 days |
| Tuna (chunk light) in water, canned | 3 years | 2 to 4 days* |

| PERISHABLES | On shelf | In fridge |
|---|---|---|
| Apples | 1 to 2 days | 3 weeks |
| Baking potatoes | 2 to 3 months | do not refrigerate |
| Bananas | until ripe | 2 days |
| Cheese (mozzarella or cheddar) | always refrigerate | 3 to 6 months (unopened) |
| Eggs | always refrigerate | 3 weeks |
| Lettuce | always refrigerate | 3 to 5 days |
| Milk | always refrigerate | 4 days |
| Onions | 3 weeks to 1 month | 2 months |
| Raisins | 9 months | 18 months |

| FROZEN FOODS | In freezer | In fridge after thawing |
|---|---|---|
| Breads | 2 months | |
| Butter | 9 months | 1 week |
| Chicken | 6 months | 1 day |
| Fish and shellfish | 3 months | 1 to 2 days |
| French fries | 6 months | 1 day |
| Ground beef | 2 to 3 months | 1 to 2 days |
| Ice cream | 1 month | |
| Vegetables | 8 months | 3 to 4 days |

* Remove these foods from cans and place in clean, airtight, nonmetallic containers.

serving platters that have held raw meat, fish, or poultry. When grilling, don't serve meat on the same platter that you used to carry it outside before cooking. If your kitchen counter comes in contact with even a drop of juice from uncooked meat, poultry, or fish, clean up the area with hot, soapy water and paper towels—not the sponge you use daily. To kill all the germs, however, you'll need to clean the surface with a mild bleach solution (one part bleach to nine parts water) or use a commercial disinfectant. Keep all kitchen surfaces dry; bacteria survive no more than a few hours when moisture is eliminated.

Even your kitchen sponges and dish-cloths—the very items that are supposed to help you get rid of lurking germs—can be part of the problem unless you clean them regularly. You should replace your sponges every two weeks. Regularly throw dishcloths in the washing machine—and always use hot water and bleach.

Experts recommend using a plastic cutting board (not wood) for raw meats —it is less likely to harbor bacteria. Wash it in hot, soapy water after each use.

## KEEPING GERMS AT BAY

Always eat food while it's hot, and refrigerate leftovers promptly. Prepared or cut food, including fruit, should not sit unrefrigerated for more than two hours in cool weather, one hour when it's warm. If the food item has been left out, toss it. Always store eggs in the fridge, and discard those with cracked or broken shells. Resist the urge to taste-test if you're unsure about something—even a small amount of contaminated food can make you very ill. Put dates on leftovers in the fridge so that you can use them within a safe period of time—usually a few days. Determining a food's safety by odor or appearance is risky; spoilage isn't always obvious.

Finally, wash produce before you eat or cook it, to remove surface germs. That way, you won't contaminate other surfaces after touching these foods. (For a list of food safety tips, see page 133.)

# SIMPLY PUT...

### HOUSEHOLD MICROBES

These three broad categories of tiny living organisms can threaten your family's health. Good hygiene and the use of a disinfectant can help keep them from causing illness.

**bacteria** • Toxic or disease-causing microorganisms such as salmonella, staph, E. coli, and Campylobacter, all of which live inside eggs and on the surface of raw meats, chicken, and shellfish.

**mildew** • Fungi that often appear as a whitish coating with a dank smell on damp towels, in bathtubs, and inside humidifiers and air conditioners; often associated with allergies.

**viruses** • Tiny infectious agents that cause colds, flu, and diseases such as hepatitis A (found in raw shellfish and in food that an infected person has handled) and Norwalk virus (found in raw shellfish from warm waters).

# AVOIDING HOUSEPLANT HEADACHES

————— ✳ —————

HOUSEPLANTS CONTRIBUTE A LOT TO YOUR HOME: BEAUTY, SERENITY, EVEN OXYGEN AS THEY GO ABOUT THEIR DAILY GROWTH AND FLOWERING. BUT THEIR NEED FOR CONSTANT CARE CAN ALSO BE A DRAIN ON YOUR TIME.

Can you keep houseplants healthy and vigorous even if you can barely spare a minute to care for them? Yes—if you follow a few simple rules.

First, keep only those plants that you truly enjoy, and that do well in your surroundings. If your house is dark and shady, for example, stay away from all cacti and other sun lovers—in low light they'll grow spindly and misshapen. If you're often out of town, avoid plants that need frequent watering, such as ferns—they will die of thirst. The tag in a new plant's potting soil can help guide you as to how much light and water the plant needs.

Take a similar approach to plants you keep out of habit. If that scraggly cutting from Aunt Agatha's rose geranium refuses to prosper, add it to the compost; she'll forgive you. If the potted azalea that sat on your desk at your hated old job makes you miserable when you look at it, toss it.

Own fewer, larger plants instead of a lot of smaller ones. They'll make a bolder statement, and you won't need to spend as much time caring for them.

To make plant care easier, keep plants in the part of the house where they'll do best: Gather those moisture-loving plants in your humid bathroom. Then, group plants that prefer life on the dry side on the same sunny sill. That way you won't harm some as you try to keep others alive.

When it comes to watering, don't kill plants with kindness. Most actually need to dry out a bit between waterings because their roots draw air from pockets in the soil. If the soil is constantly waterlogged, the plant will suffocate and rot. To avoid

**Plants crave individual attention. Save time by having just a few large ones.**

No green thumb? No problem!
Here are a few botanical best bets
that can survive some neglect.

### Asparagus fern

*(Asparagus setaceus)* Even if its soil is bone
dry, this vigorous relative of the edible stalk
won't go into a permanent swoon.

### Cast-iron plant

*(Aspidistra elatior)* Vacation plans? Don't
fret. This plant will be healthy upon your
return—even if it's neglected for weeks.

### Chinese evergreen

*(Aglaonema modestum)* It actually prefers
the soil to dry between waterings and needs
little light to thrive in your home.

### Grape ivy

*(Cissus species)* A handsome vine with ten-
drils resembling those of grapes, this plant
adapts easily to limited light and soil that's
a bit on the dry side.

### 'Janet Craig' dracaena

*(Dracaena deremensis* 'Janet Craig')* This
shrublike plant with broad leaves adapts
to low light and favors moderately dry soil.

### Ponytail

*(Beaucarnea species)* This succulent requires
little grooming and does best when not
kept too wet—just give it lots of sun and let
the soil dry between waterings.

this, wait to water until the top of the soil
dries to the liking of each type of plant.
Then water thoroughly and dump out any
excess that drains into the saucer.

If you're going on vacation, there are
several ways to keep houseplants watered
until you return. For small plants, water
and drain each one thoroughly, move it to
a shaded spot, then seal it in a plastic bag.
Or buy a capillary waterer at a plant store.
These convenient matlike or traylike devices deliver moisture to the bottoms of
pots without immersing them.

Instead of dusting those dingy leaves
by hand, place plants in the sink and gently spray them with water. Or briefly set
them in the tub under a cool (not cold)
shower until the leaves are fresh and clean.

While your houseplants are actively
growing, occasionally pinch off the last few
leaves' worth of new stems; the plants will
produce bushier, more luxuriant growth.

## Fertilize and Forget

You can worry constantly about
how much fertilizer to apply to
your houseplants—or you can
go the simple route and choose
a time-release fertilizer, available under many brand names
at most plant nurseries. Serve
up these coated pellets according to the instructions—every
four to six weeks or as infrequently as every nine months.

# PREVENTING HOUSEHOLD ACCIDENTS

———— ✳ ————

EXPECTING GUESTS—PERHAPS A VISIT FROM MOM AND DAD? OR ARE YOU GETTING READY TO WELCOME OVER SOME OF YOUR KIDS' FRIENDS? BEFORE ANYONE CROSSES YOUR THRESHOLD, CONSIDER THIS SOBERING STATISTIC:

Unintentional injury sends one of every four children to the hospital each year. Seniors and guests who are unfamiliar with your home's terrain are also at risk for accidents. You don't need to turn your home into a fortress, but there are some measures you'll want to take to minimize the chances of injury. See the tips that follow and the checklist on page 132.

## STAIRS AND WINDOWS

Make sure all walkways and stairs are clear of debris and clutter and are well lit. To prevent tots from toppling down stairs, gates that lock from banister to wall are a must. Tie up drapery and miniblind cords; they invite attention and pose a tripping or strangulation hazard for children.

Remove doors not used for privacy; they can catch little fingers. Place stickers or colored tape on sliding glass doors to keep people from crashing into them. Make sure the doors leading to hazardous rooms, such as the garage or cellar, and those leading outdoors have interior locks installed above a child's reach to prevent little ones from wandering about.

Consider replacing interior doorknobs with lever-type handles. They're easier for kids and for those whose grip is impaired.

If there's trouble, kids will find it. Search your home and root out any potential safety hazards.

## LIVING AREAS

The living room and the family room are the natural gathering areas in any home. Look carefully around these rooms for any item within reach that a toddler could knock off its perch. If you have a wobbly bookcase, fasten it securely to the wall so that a curious climber can't pull it down.

Remove all furniture with sharp corners or other protrusions, or attach foam padding to the pointed parts. Make houseplants inaccessible to babies: Some plants are poisonous, and all have leaves that can pose a choking hazard.

## KITCHEN AND BATHROOM

Since the kitchen houses a variety of sharp objects, chemicals, and choking hazards, you'll need to be especially vigilant here. Keep the telephone number for your local poison-control center close at hand, and have a bottle of syrup of ipecac to induce vomiting when—and *only* when—you are advised to do so by a physician.

## Lighting the Way

To make sure your guests are safe at night should they need to wander into the kitchen for a glass of milk, leave a small flashlight near the guest bed or in plain sight on a dresser top. They'll feel better, too, knowing they won't wake their hosts by turning on the overhead lights.

In both the kitchen and bathroom, use childproof locks to secure cabinets with cleaners inside. Do the same for drawers containing sharp tools. Stow trash containers in a locked cabinet.

> **Clear everything from around the tub. Close the toilet lid and the bathroom door after each use. An inch of water is enough to drown a small child.**

If you have a gas stove, cover the knobs with inexpensive plastic sheaths (available at children's toy and furniture stores), so only you can turn on the gas. Move refrigerator magnets out of a child's reach. If one of these breaks, its various parts could pose a choking hazard.

The bathroom is rife with danger. You can stop accidents before they happen by placing a nonslip mat on the floor of the tub or shower. Pad the bathtub spout with an insulating cover that protects against bruising and scalding. Always keep razors, blow-dryers, and other electric appliances unplugged when they're not being used. Finally, set your hot-water heater to a temperature no higher than 120°F (49°C).

Clear everything from around the bathtub. Close the toilet lid and the bathroom door after each use. Even an inch of water is enough to drown a small child.

If small children are only occasional visitors to your home, before they arrive focus on securing a single room for them to use. Remember, however, that there is no substitute for adult supervision.

# CHILDPROOFING

✳

Y OU NEEDN'T SPEND A LOT OF TIME OR MONEY to keep children safe while they're inside your home. There's a variety of simple and inexpensive add-ons that can help secure your home's danger hot spots. For more ideas, see the checklist on page 134.

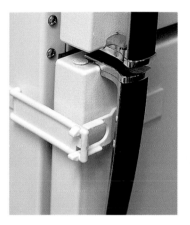

**Economical plastic latches** *for the toilet seat, refrigerator door, and kitchen and bathroom cabinets keep curious tots away from water, heavy objects, and other household hazards. Adults can still gain access to these areas and appliances: A flip of a switch, is all it takes to disengage the safety mechanisms.*

**Make bath-time safety** *fun by adding a colorful nonslip tub mat as well as a comical spout cover. A plastic swivel seat will keep your little one sitting pretty. Still, never take your eyes off a bathing baby.*

# GRIME-fighting
# Hints

**1** Break down the big weekly **chores** into smaller tasks and tackle them during the week; handle only the spillover tasks on the weekend. **2** Make your cleaning time fun. Turn on your favorite tunes and **whistle** while you work. **3** Stock cleaning **supplies** in the kitchen and bathrooms, so they'll be handy. **4** Take it with you. Put your cleaning arsenal for living areas in a lightweight **caddy** that's easy to tote from room to room. **5** Read product labels so you can choose the **right cleaner** for the soils and surfaces in your home. **6** Let the cleaning product do the **dirty work.** Spray tough spots and stains and let the cleaner work its magic while you do something else. **7** **To air out** is divine. Throw open the windows daily—fresh air shows germs an exit and makes a home smell fresher. **8** When time is short, **speed-clean** your surfaces using an all-purpose cleaner and disinfectant. **9** **Break down** holiday and spring-cleaning projects into smaller jobs you can tackle throughout the year. **10** If you can't squeeze in the time for regular or deep cleanings, bring in the **professionals.** ●

# COMING CLEAN

**MAKING SHORT WORK OF HOUSECLEANING**

*—✳—*

With work, kids, and leisure pursuits all competing for your attention, cleaning house understandably may not be your priority. Still, if you're like most people, you consider a reasonably clean home to be one of life's essentials.

So with limited time available, why devote any more of it to cleaning than is absolutely necessary? Even if you abhor a vacuum (or a broom or a mop), you can do it right—and fast. There are simple yet effective techniques for vacuuming, dusting, window cleaning, and polishing that can shave precious moments off your cleaning time. Even spring cleaning, that top-to-bottom ritual embraced by good housekeepers everywhere, is still possible on a time budget. With today's new, more effective cleaning products and tools designed to help you get the dirty jobs done at lightning speed, coming clean has never been easier—or more stress free.

It takes just a few moments to create a realistic cleaning schedule that will yield a housefull of spotless results. And you'll find that when your home sparkles, you shine too.

# HOUSECLEANING 101

——— ✳ ———

WHAT IS IT ABOUT HOUSECLEANING THAT CAN SEND EVEN THE MOST ENERGETIC AND EFFICIENT OF SOULS DUCKING FOR COVER? IF YOU'D RATHER VISIT THE DENTIST THAN DO BATTLE WITH DIRT, YOU'RE NOT ALONE.

If you cringe at the thought of tackling the mildew in the shower, chasing dust bunnies around the living room, or washing the grimy refrigerator shelves, you have a lot of company. The squeaky-clean truth is that most of us would prefer to do just about anything rather than take on the dirty jobs around the home.

Mom probably taught you the basics of housecleaning, and many of her techniques are still the most efficient today: Pick up the clutter before you clean. Dust from top to bottom. Wipe up spills as soon as they happen. But things have changed a lot since you and your mom shared living

quarters. There are many new specialty surfaces in today's home, and there is such a confusing array of specialized cleaning products on the market that it often seems easier to use the old tools and methods— or put off the job altogether. Nevertheless, it's time to come clean. But how?

## THE PERFECT PRODUCTS

The first objective is to choose the correct cleaning products for your home. Take a look at the surfaces around your house. Is there cooking grease on the stove? Mildew on the shower door? A rust stain around the tub fixture? Identifying the dirt you

When the dust bunnies start to take over, it's time to clean.

see and anticipating the germs you don't see are the first steps in determining which products you'll need to get the jobs done without damaging the surfaces.

Product labels are your best source of information. All-purpose cleaner; oven cleaner; tub, sink, and tile cleaner—the name usually says exactly what the product will do. If the name doesn't tell you, the label on the back will. Here you'll find the types of soils and surfaces the product can—or can't—be used on.

Next, consider your style of cleaning. Are you a once-a-month, bucket-wielding cleaner? If so, you'll want to stock up on the heavy-duty cleaners designed to tackle tough dirt and grime. If you prefer more frequent, quick cleanups—the simplest way to keep cleaning time to the absolute minimum—the mild all-purpose cleaners and a couple of site-specific cleaners, such as a toilet-bowl disinfectant and a tub, sink, and tile cleaner, are all you'll need to keep the surfaces in your home sparkling. Here's a list of the essentials:

◆ NONABRASIVE, ALL-PURPOSE CLEANER, IDEALLY IN A SPRAY BOTTLE

◆ TOILET-BOWL CLEANER

◆ DISINFECTANT (TRY ¾ CUP [180ML] CHLORINE BLEACH PER GALLON [4L] OF WATER)

◆ TUB, TILE, AND SINK CLEANER

◆ A BOTTLE OF LIQUID DISHWASHING DETERGENT

◆ WINDOW AND GLASS CLEANER IN A SPRAY BOTTLE

For those who prefer "natural" or environmentally friendly substitutes, the choices are mushrooming. Not only are suppliers

# SIMPLY PUT...

## CLEANING PRODUCTS

Do you need an all-purpose or a disinfectant cleaner? What's the best thing for scrubbing your tub? Listed below are some useful definitions for varieties of household cleaning products.

**all-purpose cleaners** • These mild- to middle-strength cleaners are effective on moderately soiled washable surfaces, including cabinets, floors, stove tops, painted walls, countertops, and woodwork. Some all-purpose cleaners will also disinfect.

**bathtub, tile, and sink cleaners** • These are formulated to remove soils commonly found on bathroom and kitchen surfaces, as well as hard-water deposits, soap scum, rust stains, and discolorations due to mold and mildew growth.

**cleansers** • These include more abrasive, harsher chemicals than those found in most household cleaners. They're designed for deep cleaning of stubborn stains and messes. Many contain chlorine bleach for disinfecting. Use with care; they can scratch, fade, or otherwise damage surfaces.

**disinfectant cleaners** • These and chlorine bleach are the only household cleaning substances that will kill surface bacteria and viruses. In order for a cleaning product to have the word *disinfectant* on its label, it must meet government specifications for effectiveness in killing microorganisms.

creating new "earth-friendly" cleaners, but traditional products are containing more natural ingredients. An alternative list of cleaning supplies might include:

◆ BAKING SODA WITH WATER, AS AN ALL-PURPOSE CLEANER

◆ WHITE DISTILLED VINEGAR DILUTED IN WATER, TO CLEAN WINDOWS

◆ BORAX, TO CLEAN AND DEODORIZE AND TO REMOVE TOILET-BOWL STAINS

◆ NATURAL SOAPS (CASTILE OR GLYCERIN-BASED), TO WASH DISHES

A few things to consider when choosing between so-called natural and synthetic products: Whether naturally or artificially derived, all ingredients—even water—are chemicals. There are no nontoxic sub-stances. Even salt can be deadly if taken in too high a dose. (Also, some cleaning products—notably bleach and ammonia —are dangerous when mixed. Read and follow precautions on product labels.)

Store-bought household products are required to meet standards for safe disposal down your drain, but alternative cleaning products aren't evaluated in that context. Commercial products consistently out-perform their home-mixture counterparts. Homemade cleaners generally require a great deal more time and elbow grease. The single exception is home-mixed glass cleaner: $1/4$ cup (60ml) of vinegar in $3 3/4$ cups (900ml) of warm water.

Once you've assembled your cleaning products, build a user-friendly "tool kit." The following items will maximize the effectiveness of your cleaners—and will minimize your scrubbing time:

◆ COTTON RAGS, ALL-COTTON DIAPERS, OR WHITE PAPER TOWELS

◆ SCRUBBER SPONGE

◆ LARGE SCRUB BRUSH

◆ RUBBER GLOVES

◆ SQUEEGEE

## SIMPLE TECHNIQUES

Dust and dirt begone! Here are basic tips you can employ to make your cleaning routine time-efficient but thorough:

*Voracious vacuuming.* There really is more to vacuuming than just plugging in the machine and giving your rug or carpet a once-over. To suck up all the dirt and dust hidden between the fibers, you need to spend about 20 seconds or so going back and forth over each area of the rug.

# STASHING TOOLS AND SUPPLIES

❋

CLEANUPS, WHETHER QUICK OR THOROUGH, are much easier when tools and supplies are readily accessible. Stock up on the essentials—brooms, mops, scrubbers, cleaners, rags, and paper towels—then store and carry them so that they'll always be on hand where you need them. Here are some simple suggestions.

**A supply caddy,** *available at many stores, makes it easy to tote all you need from room to room. When you have a moment to clean, just pick up and go. Or create two holders—one for kitchen and bath, the other for living areas—each filled with room-specific supplies.*

**Wooden pegs** *affixed to a wall in the utility area keep bulky cleaning tools together while maximizing space. A hanging net bag is a handy place to store rags or sponges that are still partially damp. Later, use it to haul them to the washing machine.*

**Lidded plastic boxes** *organize polishes, buffing cloths, and other small items that would get lost or jumbled on a cabinet shelf. The boxes are easy to carry where they're needed.*

# HOUSECLEANING TIMETABLE

✳

HOW OFTEN SHOULD YOU TACKLE various housekeeping chores? The answer depends on how fastidious you are, how much time you have to clean, and how active your family is in your home. Here's a general plan that can help you put your housecleaning on a yearlong schedule. For easy reference, make a copy of this chart and post it where you store your major cleaning supplies.

| | Daily | Weekly | Monthly | Quarterly | Semi-annually | Annually |
|---|---|---|---|---|---|---|
| **HOUSEWIDE** | | | | | | |
| Wash windows | | | | ● | | |
| Vacuum carpets | | ● | | | | |
| Shampoo carpets | | | | | ● | |
| Reseal wood floors | | | | | | ● |
| Dust | | ● | | | | |
| Clean ceiling fixtures | | | | | | ● |
| Wash walls and baseboards | | | | ● | | |
| | | | | | | |
| **KITCHEN** | | | | | | |
| Wash dishes | ● | | | | | |
| Disinfect countertops | | ● | | | | |
| Rinse kitchen sink | ● | | | | | |
| Mop floor | | ● | | | | |
| Clean refrigerator shelves | | | ● | | | |
| Clean refrigerator coils | | | | ● | | |
| | | | | | | |
| **BEDROOMS** | | | | | | |
| Make beds | ● | | | | | |
| Change bed linens | | ● | | | | |
| Vacuum and turn mattresses | | | | | ● | |
| | | | | | | |
| **BATHROOMS** | | | | | | |
| Clean toilet | | ● | | | | |
| Clean shower or tub | | ● | | | | |
| Squeegee shower (or sponge tub) | ● | | | | | |
| Mop floors | | ● | | | | |
| | | | | | | |
| **UTILITY AREAS** | | | | | | |
| Disinfect indoor trash cans | | | ● | | | |

For those neat vacuum patterns in the rug that announce, "I've been cleaned!" pretend you're mowing the lawn. Divide the area into strips and tackle each strip in sections using a back-and-forth motion. This last step is purely for appearances; your rug will be just as clean if you vacuum in a random pattern.

*Fabulously clean furniture.* To get your furniture and hardwood surfaces shining, you don't need fancy cleaners. They often leave a residue that will attract more dust than if you hadn't used them. Instead of a fancy product in a spray bottle, use soft cotton or terry, a 100 percent cotton diaper, or a cleaning cloth (you'll find these cloths in the cleaning product section of your grocery store). Lightly moisten the cloth with water and gently buff the surface along the grain. This technique will remove most spills and fingerprints.

There is an easy way to remove white water rings and marks from oil-finished woods such as teak: Coat the spot with a thick film of cooking oil, then gently rub with fine steel wool or a light-duty plastic scrubber until the stain fades. Buff the area with a clean cloth or soft paper towel.

## EXTRA SPARKLE

*Mirror, mirror on the wall.* For streak- and spot-free glass you'll need a squeegee; a glass cleaner; and a clean, lint-free rag. Spray the glass cleaner lightly on the rag and wash the surface; using horizontal strokes to prevent dripping, squeegee it dry. For extra sparkle, polish the surface when it's nearly dry with a piece of newspaper. The ink used in some papers may

## Dust Busters

Don't just move dust from one place to another—capture and remove it. The feather duster your mom may have used sent dust into the air, but the dust eventually settled back down where it came from. Today's more effective tools of choice: a vacuum attachment to suck up the dirt and allergens, or simply a dampened clean cloth to which the fluffy stuff sticks.

smudge the glass when it's wet, so try this first in a small area before attempting to buff the entire surface.

*Sparkling silver and silver plate.* You'll need silver polish—either a commercial brand or ordinary toothpaste will work. Put a bit of the polish on a damp cloth or a clean cotton sock (socks make ideal polishing cloths—apply polish with one side; then turn the sock over and buff with the other side). Use up-and-down rather than circular strokes to polish the item quickly and effectively in less time. Use a twisted bit of rag to get between silverware tines and other tight spaces. Finish the job with a few strokes using a clean, dry cloth (or the clean side of the sock).

Store silver behind glass, in cloth or plastic bags, or in plastic wrap to keep tarnish to a minimum. Resist the urge to bundle your silver in rubber bands: rubber can cause discoloration.

# THE CLEANING ROUTINE

---- ✳ ----

U NTIL SOMEONE OUT THERE INTRODUCES A UNIVERSALLY FREE HOUSEHOLD
CLEANING SERVICE, MOST OF US WILL CONTINUE TO TACKLE THE LESS-
THAN-THRILLING TASK OF CLEANING OUR OWN HOMES EACH WEEK.

Still, you can make this routine task more pleasant, and shave precious moments off your overall cleaning time in the process.

A few tricks to get you off the couch and into the cleaning routine: Pump up the volume on your CD player, or pop a book-on-tape into the cassette player. Pick up some stylish new cleaning tools at the store; your curiosity about a new product may get you moving. For a housecleaning timetable, see page 54.

## ROOM SERVICE

The way Mom taught you to do dishes—wash lightly soiled cups and plates first, scrub the dinner pans with baked-on food last—works equally well for cleaning your home's surfaces. Scrubbing with murky water or soiled sponges redistributes dirt instead of removing it. Start cleaning in the lightly soiled bedrooms, dining room, and living room. After you've completed those areas—and with a sense of accomplishment—work your way into the more challenging kitchen and bathroom.

The major culprits found in the bedrooms, dining room, and living room are dust, tracked-in dirt, and clutter. In each of these rooms, you'll use essentially the same method to clean.

Move clockwise around each room, putting away surface clutter or mislaid items. Stash outside the door any stuff that doesn't belong in the room.

Then dust shelves, windowsills, miniblinds, lamps, tables, bureaus, and TV screens with a clean, damp cloth. (Dusting with a dry cloth can eventually scratch or dull the finish on porous surfaces such as wood.) When you run out of clean areas on the rag, either get a fresh cloth or rinse the used one clean, then twist it dry to remove any excess water.

Make your mirrors and windows shine using glass cleaner (or a vinegar-and-water solution) and a squeegee.

Vacuum upholstered chairs and sofas, and take decorative pillows outdoors to

## Let Cleaners Do the Dirty Work

Don't scrub! Most of today's tough, quick-acting cleaners can do most of the dirty work without much help from you. Simply spray or wipe cleaner on the tub or toilet and wait several minutes for it to do its work. Wipe clean with a rag or paper towel.

shake the dust and airborne dirt out of them—or fluff them up with a 10-minute tumble in the dryer. Vacuum-clean curtains or drapes. Change bedroom linens.

Finish each room with a quick surface vacuuming, and spend a few extra seconds vacuuming near the doorways.

## SEVEN SIMPLE STEPS

Kitchens are a potluck of dirt, grease, and germs. For this room you'll need an all-purpose cleaner; a disinfectant cleaner; a glass cleaner (or a vinegar-and-water mix); dishwashing detergent; a clean, dry cloth; a scrubber sponge; and a scourer (the ball-shaped, woven-plastic kind that resembles the copper scourers of the past but doesn't scratch today's modern surfaces).

The following seven-step method, which begins with decluttering and ends with mopping your way out the door, is simpler than Mom's equally effective but time-consuming method—there are no double buckets or serious scrubbing here. Instead, you treat the prime surfaces that need weekly attention, letting the specialized cleaners do much of the dirty work for you. Then your job is simply to go back and wipe all the surfaces clean.

## Clockwise Cleaning

This smart approach ensures that you'll attend to a room's every surface in a single pass. Begin at the door and clean from top to bottom, moving clockwise around each room. This pushes the dust toward the floor as you work, to be vacuumed or swept away last.

*Step one.* Declutter. Put away anything that's out of place, such as dishes languishing in the sink or the kids' homework on the kitchen table, and remove everything from the counters. Send oven mitts and dishtowels into the wash. Toss anything from the fridge that's past its prime (see page 41 for guidelines) or that the troops are unlikely to consume.

*Step two.* Spot patrol. Don't waste your precious time scrubbing dried-on foods or baked-on spills on the countertops and the stove; instead, give them a generous spritz of all-purpose cleaner. Allow the cleaner to penetrate the grime while you move on.

**Big cleaning jobs call for tools that are up to the challenge.**

## Controlling Carpet Odor

If you've vacuumed your carpet and it still doesn't smell as fresh as you'd like it to, grab a box of baking soda from your kitchen shelf. Sprinkle it liberally over the entire carpet and let it sit for 15 minutes—or overnight if the floor covering is seriously smelly. Vacuum the powder up the next morning.

*Step three.* Soak it up. Fill the sink with hot, soapy water and place your stove-burner rings and vent-hood filter inside to soak for at least 15 or 20 minutes to soften the baked-on food spills and splatters. (Your dishwasher could scratch the decorative surface of some burner rings.)

*Step four.* Oven duty. Open the (cool) oven and remove the oven racks. Scrape off any burned-on stains with a dull knife held at a 30-degree angle. Use an oven cleaner for manually cleaned ovens; if you have a self-cleaning oven, simply turn it on and let the appliance clean itself. Don't use an oven cleaner in a self-cleaning or continuous-cleaning oven, however; it may damage the surface. To eliminate the need for frequent deep cleanings in the future, sponge away oven spills before they dry or are burned to a crisp.

For baked-on messes in the microwave, apply hand dishwashing detergent using your scrubber sponge; rinse clean.

*Step five.* Surface duty. After you've obliterated the baked-on messes in the oven, work your way around the kitchen cleaning the other surfaces. First, wipe up the spots you sprayed in step two; then use an all-purpose cleaner for a general wipe-down of countertops, the oven exterior, cabinets, dishwasher, and refrigerator. To

**Move methodically** *as you clean, from ceiling to counters to floor, working clockwise around the room. Finish at the doorway.*

prevent streak marks when cleaning large vertical areas such as appliance surfaces, start at the bottom and work up, overlapping areas with a circular motion. Rinse the sponge and reapply cleaner frequently.

By making one thorough cleaning trip around the room, you're sure to hit all the surface hot spots. Finish by spraying a disinfectant cleaner on the countertops and refrigerator handle, allowing the cleaner to sit for at least 10 minutes.

*Step six.* Finishing touches. Retrieve the vent-hood filter and stove-burner rings that are soaking in the sink; sponge them clean of any lingering grime; rinse, dry, and put them back in place. Clean the sink and faucet with a sponge and dishwashing liquid or all-purpose cleaner to remove any residue. To make the faucet sparkle, spritz it with a glass cleaner and polish dry. Wipe the countertops and refrigerator door handle clean of disinfectant.

*Step seven.* Floor time. Sweep first to get rid of corner crumbs and then mop with a floor-care product designed for your floor type. Keep in mind that flooring can become cloudy with built-up residue from cleaning solution, so be sure to rinse well after each cleaning. Better still: Use a no-rinse floor-cleaning product and simply mop your way out the kitchen door.

If you spot-clean spills immediately after they happen, your floors will stay cleaner between moppings.

## BATHROOM BASICS

Bathrooms are where cleaning challenges can get tough. With so many different surfaces—chrome, brass, glass, porcelain, and

**Put a shine** *on your shower, tub, and sink fixtures. A once-over with a glass cleaner and a polishing cloth should do nicely.*

fiberglass—it's difficult to know where to begin or what to use. But you don't need to buy baskets full of specialty cleaners to keep everything looking good. With just four basic products you can get the job done: an all-purpose cleaner; tub, tile, and sink cleaner; a toilet-bowl cleaner; and a glass cleaner. You'll also need the correct tools: a long-handled toilet brush, a scrubber sponge, a dust cloth, and paper towels.

You can save time by spraying cleaners on areas that will benefit from some extra soaking time—such as the toilet and tub or the shower—and tackling other surfaces while the cleaners do their stuff. The simple seven-step method that follows will have you in and out—and your bathroom buffed—in minutes rather than hours. Instead of endless scrubbing, let the cleaners penetrate, so that all you have to do on

**Bathroom surfaces** *are highly specialized—washable walls, ceramic tile, porcelain—so be sure to use the proper cleaner for each.*

most surfaces is wipe them clean. Begin where the bulk of bathroom germs lurk—the toilet bowl—and surface-clean your way around the room.

*Step one.* Sanitize the bowl. Squeeze some of the toilet-bowl cleaner around the inside of the bowl and under the rim. Use a long-handled toilet brush to swish the cleaner around the bowl, under the rim, and as far into the trap as possible.

Let the solution stand a few minutes as you clean the seat, lid, and outside of the bowl with an all-purpose cleaner and a sponge, cloth, or paper towels. Using paper towels is the simplest—no rinsing is needed and there's no chance of spreading germs, as you'll toss out the towels immediately after use.

*Step two.* Tame the scum. Soapy build-up makes for unsightly baths. Spray the shower or tub and sink with a tub, tile, and sink cleaner. Let it sit while you complete the remaining steps.

*Step three.* Wipe the deck. Clear the countertop of personal items and spray the surface with all-purpose cleaner. Wipe clean with a sponge or paper towels. Replace your toiletries.

*Step four.* Shine it. Spray glass cleaner on a cloth and wash the mirror's surface. Squeegee dry. Use glass cleaner to make the faucet sparkle, too.

*Step five.* Dust and smudge duty. Clear shelves and dust; spot-clean wall smudges with an all-purpose cleaner and sponge. Give full attention to areas around light switches and doorknobs.

*Step six.* Surface scrubbing. Use a scrubber sponge to loosen and remove soap scum and buildup on the tub or shower. Rinse clean, thus completing step two. To make your job easier in the future, keep a squeegee in the shower or a sponge in the tub for quick wipe-downs of the shower walls and door or the sides of the tub to help prevent soap-scum buildup.

**Break down the big jobs into small, manageable tasks, and tackle them day by day. Clean the microwave Monday, the toilet Tuesday, the floors Wednesday.**

To keep mildew in check, open the shower door or curtain after use to let it air-dry. If mildew already has a toehold, scrub the surface with ¾ cup (180ml) of bleach in 1 gallon (4L) of water; rinse clean.

*Step seven*. Vacuum or sweep. Then mop the floor clean. Empty the trash can and take the bag with you as you go.

## SPEED-CLEANING

Even if you don't have a lot of time to spend cleaning, you can do it right—and fast. Most important, cleaning "lite" can lift your spirits just as much as if you had attacked the place with your most thorough cleaning regimen.

Shift into high gear by stocking up on supplies for the quick-and-dirty jobs that lie ahead. Gather cleaners, rags, paper towels, sponge, and scrub brush in the kitchen and bath so you won't have to backtrack between rooms to get what you need. By keeping a permanent stash of supplies in each of these rooms, you'll always be prepared to tackle those last-minute cleanups quickly and efficiently.

Break down the big jobs into small, manageable tasks, and tackle them day by day. Clean the microwave Monday, the toilet Tuesday. Mop the floors Wednesday, tackle the tub Thursday. By Friday, your big target areas—the kitchen and bath-room—are nearly done. A few minutes spent Friday on surface duty, and your home is clean—and the weekend is yours.

You can also quicken the pace of your weekly cleaning routine by focusing on a different type of cleaning each week. Choose an all-purpose cleaner this Friday, and spend several minutes spritzing and wiping the main surfaces of your kitchen and bathroom. Use a disinfectant cleaner next Friday, spraying on countertops, in toilets, and in the tub or shower. Then go read the mail or relax; return to flush the toilet and wipe clean the countertops and tub or shower. Dust this week, vacuum the next. This simple routine means no juggling of cloths and paper towels, switching of spray bottles, or putting away of dust rags as you pull out the vacuum. You focus on just one thing at a time.

If you've got better things to do this week—or you simply can't summon the energy for housework—it's OK to take a break from your cleaning routine. Going two weeks between disinfecting and dusting won't cause any irreparable harm, and taking a rest may do you good.

The faster you can zip through housework,
the more time you'll have to relax.

# Spring and Holiday Cleaning

---✳---

DOES SPRING-CLEANING—THAT ANNUAL RITE OF HOME PURIFICATION EMBRACED BY NEATNIKS AND GOOD HOUSEKEEPERS EVERYWHERE—STILL HAVE A PLACE IN THE TIME-CRUNCHED, TWO-CAREER HOUSEHOLD OF TODAY?

Absolutely. No matter how busy you are —or perhaps *because* your home seems to have a revolving door—the annual purging of a year's worth of mildew, grime, dust, and dirt still needs to be done so you can get by with simple surface cleanings the rest of the year. And if friends and family visit your home during other times, such as the winter holidays, this top-to-bottom buffing is even more essential. They may *say* they don't notice—but don't you take note of a home's dusty shelves and dingy floors when you visit?

A thorough cleaning not only begets a sparkling-clean house, it can also help your appliances last longer. But you don't have to spend your entire weekend with broom and sponge in hand to get your home perked up with springtime cheer or primed for holiday entertaining.

## SPRING INTO ACTION

The key to getting it all done in less time is to break the chores down into manageable loads, then tackle them over several weeks or even months—that is, unless you're the type who likes to schedule a weekend sequestered indoors with mops and brooms. This less-traditional bit-by-bit approach will reward you with the

same old-fashioned feeling that keeps the spring-cleaning ritual alive: pride in your healthful, well-maintained home.

Start by focusing your efforts on the big pieces and on the places that make the most difference to you: furnishings, appliances, and carpeting. Also take stock of which cleaning tasks you can forgo. The following essentials will have your home spring-cleaned in no time:

*Make doormats welcoming.* Shake 'em, wash 'em, swat 'em with a broom. Give them the toughest cleaning they can take. They're your front line against tracked-in dirt—so keep them clean enough to function at peak efficiency.

*Clean carpets and upholstery.* Fabrics that have absorbed a winter's worth of dirt, body oil, and germs will need a deep cleaning to get them ready for another year of wear—and for that close inspection by your relaxing guests.

When you're shampooing carpets or cleaning upholstery with a rented carpet cleaner, practice first in an unobtrusive area to make sure that you have the knack of the machine and that the treatment won't discolor fabrics or cause dyes to run. Save time by moving furniture just slightly —not out of the room or against the wall, as the old rules dictated—and place the legs of each piece back on top of small waxed paper squares after shampooing. The waxed paper will protect your carpet and keep the furniture legs from getting wet as the carpet dries. Open the windows to speed the drying process, which can take a day or more. If you're not the furniture-shifting and machine-renting type, make it easy on yourself. Call in a professional carpet and upholstery cleaner to do the work and take the morning off.

*Finish your floors.* To protect the floors in your kitchen from another year of wear and tear, wax or apply a sealer following label directions. The simplest method: Use a combination wash-and-wax floor cleaner. Don't feel guilty about saving time!

No-wax floors don't need a polishing treatment, but an occasional makeover will keep them looking fresher—and add

a protective buffer that could help them last longer. Use a floor cleaner that cleans, shines, or both. It's best to follow label directions for proper use of each product.

**If you're not the furniture-shifting and machine-renting type, make it easy on yourself. Call in a professional carpet cleaner and take the morning off.**

If you have wood floors, move furniture and rugs aside, then apply a wood cleaner and either liquid or paste polish to clean and add a new wax coating.

*Wash walls, cabinets, baseboards, and woodwork.* The walls may not look as if they need a bath—after all, dust and soot fall to the floor, right? Most of it does, but just enough clings to vertical surfaces to warrant a seasonal or preholiday bath. Use a sponge and hand dishwashing detergent, washing the surface in sections. A sponge mop makes it easier to reach higher spots. Use two buckets: one for the dishwashing detergent solution and another for wringing out your sponge. Dry the walls and woodwork with a clean cloth.

*Vacuum with intelligence.* The old rules mandated that you go through the labor-intensive task of dragging every stick of

to the left or to the right. Vacuum the area previously occupied by the furniture and then move it back into place.

*Clean ceiling fixtures.* Remove dust and dirt from ceiling fans and air-conditioner vents with a cloth and a vacuum with a soft nozzle attachment.

*Clean your light fixtures.* A few minutes with a stepladder, an all-purpose cleaner, a sponge, and a polish cloth will give new light to your life. If your home has sky-

**For skylights or tall ceilings, invest in extended-reach dust- and dirt-removal tools, available at hardware and janitorial-supply stores.**

furniture off the carpet, just so the vacuum cleaner could cover every nook and cranny. The new rules will save you time, and you'll still get the corner-to-corner cleaning done: Simply move big items a little

**Stairways can be** *dramatic when the woodwork gleams from polishing and the stairs are dust-free from a thorough vacuuming.*

lights or tall ceilings, consider investing in a stepladder and extended-reach dust- and dirt-removal tools, all of which are available at your local hardware store and at home- and janitorial-supply stores.

*Check your coils.* You should clean the refrigerator's condenser coil, usually found behind the toe grille, with a long-handled bottle brush and a vacuum cleaner with an attachment hose to remove dust and lint. Built-up dust can shut down the unit by causing it to overheat.

To remove dust from coils attached to the hard-to-reach back side of the fridge, carefully pull the refrigerator out several feet (newer models roll on casters) and vacuum thoroughly; finish by sweeping or vacuuming the floor area you've revealed. Expect to rediscover coins, bottle caps, and twist ties that you and the cat knocked there over the past year.

Once you've covered these major hot spots in your home, you'll have spring or holiday cleaning all wrapped up.

# BRINGING IN THE PROS

---　✳　---

I F EVEN WEEKLY CLEANINGS ARE TOUGH TO SQUEEZE IN—LET ALONE THE BIG SEASONAL AND HOLIDAY JOBS—HOW CAN YOU POSSIBLY GET YOUR HOME CLEAN? THE ANSWER: BRING IN THE PROFESSIONALS.

These soap-and-bucket veterans will handle everything from washing windows and miniblinds to deep-cleaning carpets, floors, and drapery. They'll tackle your home's most formidable tasks—or those you simply abhor—and leave you with clean and well-maintained surroundings.

You have two options: specialists—for floors, windows, upholstery, carpets, or drapery—and general housecleaning services that tackle all these tasks and more on a weekly, monthly, or as-needed basis.

Which is better for you? If you require help throughout the house, a cleaning service is the most efficient way to go. Most services include complete floor-to-ceiling, room-by-room cleaning—many will even make up unmade beds.

Most companies are flexible, so if you have a specific task you need done, ask. If given enough notice, most services are usually quite happy to do everything from the ironing and laundry to cleaning out the inside of the refrigerator and kitchen cabinets. You'll probably have to pay for the extra time these tasks will take, but buying yourself some freedom from such small but necessary jobs will keep your home running smoothly and can be well worth the investment.

If the only thing you don't do is windows, however, hire a professional window cleaner. Ditto for the floors, carpets, and upholstery. These site-specific professionals have the latest tools, products, and industry know-how to guide them to the very best methods to clean these surfaces. Of course, general housecleaning services will handle most of these chores, but you may want to ask how extensively workers have performed each job in the past.

See page 136 for a list of questions you might want to ask housecleaning professionals, whether they'll be cleaning your whole house or focusing on a specific area.

**In a pinch** *or on a regular basis, cleaning specialists can tackle the jobs that are too tough—or time-consuming—for you alone.*

# STEPS to
# CLEANER Clothes

---*---

**1** Immediately rinse or blot away **spills** on your clothes to prevent stains from setting. **2** Read fabric care **labels** before you wash. Your clothes will last longer if you know how to treat them.

**3** Sort **laundry** by color, wash cycle needed, and water temperature required. **4** Before washing stained garments, **pretreat** or presoak the spot. If at first you don't succeed, wash, wash again. **5** To keep **snags and lint** to a minimum, zip zippers, button buttons, empty pockets, and brush away lint before tossing duds in the hamper. **6** If your clothing is heavily **soiled,** your load large, or the water cold, add extra detergent. **7** Add fabric softener for **fluffier** clothes. **8** Check **wet** garments for remaining stains, and re-treat as needed before drying. Heat will set stains.

**9** Dry only **full loads.** Tumbling a handful of garments prolongs the drying time by reducing the tumbling. **10** Leave **tough** stains and delicate fabrics for the dry cleaner. ●

# FIGHTING THE WASH-DAY BLUES

## EXPERT TIPS FOR LIGHTENING YOUR LOAD

\* —— \*\* —— \*

No matter how busy you are each week, chances are high that laundry is the one routine task that usually gets done. After all, it's hard to ignore a pile of soiled clothing when you're fresh out of workout shorts or your kids don't have a clean pair of socks to wear to school.

But if you've ever pulled a pink shirt out of the washing machine when a white one went in, or put on a fresh pair of jeans that are still sporting the signs of last week's picnic, you know that even a simple task you've done hundreds of times can get complicated now and then.

By following the basic sorting techniques, matching the right laundry products and water temperature to each load, and putting stain-busting strategies into play, you can make such spotty moments disappear. You'll be rewarded with clothes that look cleaner and actually last longer, and you'll have more time to tackle other jobs you've been neglecting.

# Laundry ABCs

---*---

DON'T FEEL GUILTY IF YOU'VE FORGOTTEN THE LAUNDRY BASICS THAT MOM TAUGHT YOU. THIS REFRESHER COURSE WILL HAVE YOU SORTING CLOTHES, SELECTING DETERGENT, AND SETTING THE MACHINE LIKE A PRO IN NO TIME.

Your studious efforts in the laundry room will be rewarded with clean, bright clothes that would make your mother proud.

Success in the laundry room requires simple preparation. Sure, the quickest way to do the laundry is to separate the whites, medium colors, and darks and to wash each load in cold water. But the time you save in the short run may actually double your wash-day workload later.

Cold water doesn't clean some dirty fabrics nearly as well as warmer temperatures; it can leave them looking dingy and worn instead of bright and clean. And, you'll be back in the store looking for new chinos or Oxford shirts sooner than if you had taken a few moments to wash them the way the manufacturers suggest.

To lighten your workload and lessen the toll that agitation takes on clothing, wash garments only when they really need it. It sounds obvious, but many of us are in the habit of washing everything we've worn each day—perhaps because it's easier to toss clothes in the hamper than to hang them up or to put them in a drawer. Of course you'll want to wash the undergarments you change each day, but give that cotton sweater or that pair of jeans a close inspection before you automatically subject it to another washing and drying.

If your duds are definitely dirty, however, get them prepped for a spin in the washing machine *before* you toss them in the clothes hamper. Wash day will go more smoothly if you do the following:

◆ ZIP ZIPPERS, SNAP SNAPS, FASTEN HOOKS, AND TIE LACES TOGETHER.

◆ TURN DOWN CUFFS ON PANTS OR SHIRTS; BRUSH AWAY DIRT AND LINT.

◆ MAKE SURE POCKETS ARE EMPTY.

◆ REMOVE BELTS, PINS, AND OTHER DECORATIONS.

◆ TURN CLOTHES INSIDE OUT TO KEEP ABRASION FROM FADING THEM.

Taking care of these odds and ends will ensure that important notes tucked in a

## Liquid Versus Powder

Which laundry detergent is best for your family? Liquid laundry detergents are especially effective on food and greasy or oily soils. Because they are fluid, they also work as pretreaters for spots and stains. Powders are ideal for general wash-day loads, effectively lifting out clay and ground-in dirt.

shirt pocket won't come out blank, and that hooks and zippers won't snag other fabrics in the wash cycle.

When should you do the laundry? Contrary to conventional wisdom, you don't have to wait for a full load. Today's energy-efficient washers let you adjust the water level to fit the load, so you needn't feel guilty about washing a few of your favorite shirts as you need them.

Whenever your wash day does roll around—whether you'll be at home or at the local laundromat—plan to stay put and make the most of your time while the washer and dryer do their job.

If you head out to the laundromat, bring some mail to sort through or catalogs to read instead of running errands while you wait. When washing at home, plan to tackle the little things around the house—or simply take time for yourself and sit down with that magazine you've been wanting to read. Resist the urge to go out and run errands—laundry that sits for several hours can get wrinkled.

## SORTING MADE SIMPLE

The secret behind getting everything clean safely is to sort your laundry into loads of similar colors, wash cycles, and water temperature needs, and to set aside stained garments for prewash TLC.

Look to the clothing care labels on your garments for guidance. They make selecting the proper machine settings simple. If you've gone shopping lately, you may have noticed that the clothing labels have changed a bit. Today's international care labels often have symbols as well as,

or instead of, words. Most of the symbols are pretty self-explanatory. An icon of an iron with dots inside tells you the proper heat setting for pressing that garment (one dot for low, three for high). A cuplike icon with dots tells you the wash temperature (one dot for cool/cold, three for hot). A simple circle indicates clothing you should

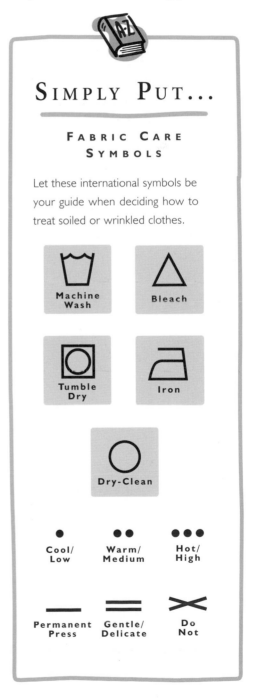

## SIMPLY PUT...

### FABRIC CARE SYMBOLS

Let these international symbols be your guide when deciding how to treat soiled or wrinkled clothes.

| | |
|---|---|
| Machine Wash | Bleach |
| Tumble Dry | Iron |
| Dry-Clean | |

| | | |
|---|---|---|
| ● | ●● | ●●● |
| Cool/ Low | Warm/ Medium | Hot/ High |
| — | = | ✕ |
| Permanent Press | Gentle/ Delicate | Do Not |

STREAMLINE THE CONTENTS OF YOUR
LAUNDRY ROOM, AND YOU'LL HAVE
QUICKER ACCESS TO ALL YOU NEED.

❖

### Utility shelving

Wall-mounted shelves help keep miscellaneous cleaning supplies from taking over the
laundry area. They're still within easy reach
when you need them. Keep duplicate items
and the products you use less frequently at
the back of the shelf.

### Notions board

Did a hem unravel? A seam rip? A button
fall off in the wash? A bulletin board on
your laundry-room wall can keep needles,
thread, scissors, extra buttons, and other
sewing supplies handy for quick repairs. Or
use the board to post notes to your kids,
spouse, or housekeeper ("Don't put my red
sweater in the dryer—it'll shrink!").

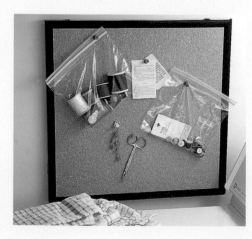

dry-clean, and a circle overlaid with an
X identifies garments that should never
be sent to the dry cleaner.

But when clothes are labeled dry-clean
only, must you obey? The dry-cleaning
industry will tell you yes, and if you can't
live without that silk blouse, you should
comply. If you clean it yourself, you risk
damage like shrinkage, color loss or fading, and fabric texture changes—silk can
lose its sheen, and linen can end up looking lumpy instead of crisp.

The benefits: If you don't mind gam-
bling, you save money and have the item
ready when you need it. Your best hand-
washing bets (cold water, please) include
plain-weave light-colored silks, cashmere
(washed inside out), fuzzy sweaters, and
fancy loose-weave knits. While dry cleaning will keep these clothes looking new
longer, some of these may be carefully
hand-washed and air-dried.

Start sorting by reading each garment's
label and separating into six piles:

◆ COLD-WATER WHITES

◆ WARM-WATER WHITES

◆ COLD-WATER PASTELS AND
  LIGHT COLORS

◆ WARM-WATER PASTELS AND
  LIGHT COLORS

◆ COLD-WATER BRIGHTS AND DARKS

◆ WARM-WATER BRIGHTS AND DARKS

Of course, six piles could translate into six
loads; if you've got the time during the
evening, this is the safest way to keep your
clothes looking good. However, if time is
short and your needs are immediate, combine and wash the cold-water pastels and

light colors with the cold-water brights and darks; do the same for your warm-water loads. But resist the temptation to mix any colors with white loads.

As you sort, be on the lookout for items that have spills or stains (see pages 75–77 for tips on removing some common stains), really grungy dungarees and kids' clothes (very dirty garments can actually transfer dirt in the wash to lightly soiled clothes), and those that require a gentle wash cycle. Create three separate stacks for these: hot water, gentle cycle, and pretreat.

Once again, you can mix things up in a pinch: If you have only a few light-colored cold- or warm-wash items that require the gentle cycle, throw in similarly colored items that need the same temperature. The add-ins won't get as clean with the gentle cycle's agitation, but it's OK to simplify your laundry life. Still, always go with the gentlest cycle and coolest temperature when you mix fabrics and colors.

**Check clothes carefully** *before tossing them into the washing machine. Certain fabrics require hand washing or dry cleaning.*

## Lifting Lint

To keep lint—short fibers and yarns loosened in the laundering process—off your clothes and out of your life, take time to sort your clothes carefully before you toss them into the washing machine. Separate lint-shedders, such as fuzzy sweatshirts, chenille robes, flannels, and towels, from lint-keepers, such as knits, corduroys, and permanent-press and synthetic fabrics. Make sure there are no tissues left in any pockets.

Be sure also to check trim and decorations for colorfastness. One red-trimmed white shirt could leave you with a load of pink clothes. Unsure? Dip a hidden corner of the fabric or an inside seam in your liquid detergent or in a mixture of your powder detergent and hot water. Rinse and let it air-dry. If the color remains unchanged, the garment is colorfast.

### HOT, WARM, OR COLD?

It's time to select a wash cycle and temperature. Let your fabrics determine the cycle if the label doesn't tell you: sturdy fabrics, such as jeans and heavy cotton shirts, get the normal or regular cycle; combinations of synthetic and natural fibers need the permanent-press cycle; sheer and delicate fabrics do best in the gentle cycle.

How important is the right temperature? It directly affects the performance of

## An Ounce of Prevention

Don't overload your washer. If clothes are packed too tightly, they won't circulate freely in the wash water and won't get completely clean.

Warm water minimizes color fading and wrinkling. Choose it for washing synthetic fibers, natural and synthetic blends, and moderately soiled fabrics.

Cold water will protect most dark or bright-colored clothing from running and minimizes shrinkage of washable woolens. Use it for lightly soiled clothes and those with blood, wine, or coffee stains (which may set if washed in warm or hot water), regardless of the fabric. If you're going to do a cold-water wash, check first for stains and spots and pretreat garments; detergent doesn't clean heavily soiled areas as well in cold water. If you do lots of cold-water washes, consider using a laundry detergent designed to work in all temperatures.

But for the rinse cycle, cold water is excellent for all types of loads. Another benefit: A cold-water rinse can reduce the energy used per load by up to one-third and minimize wrinkling in synthetic or permanent-press fabrics.

the laundry detergent, the wrinkling of fabrics, and the life span of your clothes —so follow the care labels.

If a label is not legible, remember that hot water works well on ground-in and hard-to-remove dirt on sturdy fabrics. Still, few labels recommend regular hot-water washing. Use it to clean seriously soiled garments (gardening or children's clothing), and to regularly disinfect dish towels, washcloths, bath towels, bedding, and pillowcases. This is one time you don't want to mix lights and darks, as hotter temperatures can cause some fabrics to bleed. (Whites warrant the solo treatment no matter what the temperature.)

### READY, SET, WASH

Adjust your machine's water level to correspond to your load, and make your cycle selection. Add detergent and fill the tub before you load your clothes. If your load is average (5 to 7 pounds [2–3kg]), with moderate soil, and you use warm water, follow the product's directions. Use more if the clothes are really grungy, if the load is full, or if you're using cold water.

Place clothes loosely in the washer, taking care not to wrap items around the agitator, where they could become tangled during the cycle. Know when to say when: Clothes should move freely through the water for optimum cleaning. If you're not sure, lift the lid during the cycle. Properly loaded clothes should sink and then reappear on the surface. Overloading causes clothes to rub together—breaking down the fibers—and reduces the effectiveness of your detergent; it also allows dirt to be redeposited on clothes instead of heading down the drain with the rinse water.

If you're using chlorine bleach to help your detergent brighten whites or clean heavily soiled clothes, add it to the dispenser after your wash load has agitated for about five minutes, so that the bleach can fully work its magic. Bleach assists your detergent by converting dirt into more-soluble particles.

If you're using an oxygen (color-safe) bleach, add it at the same time as you add the detergent, but put the bleach directly in the water before you add clothes, not into the bleach dispenser. The thicker liquid can clog the dispenser. Don't use both types of bleach at the same time—they can neutralize each other's effectiveness.

A simpler alternative to adding bleach is to buy and use a detergent that contains bleach (either the chlorine type or a color-safe alternative). Then you won't need to go through the extra step of adding a separate bleach to the wash—although adding a little more of the appropriate type of bleach won't hurt, either.

## TUMBLE DRY

If you have several small loads, dry them together to protect your clothes from heat damage and to hasten the drying process. Drying small loads reduces the tumbling effect produced by a pile of clothes rotating all together, and therefore actually prolongs the amount of time it can take to dry the clothes.

Set the dryer cycle to Regular or High if your load is all-cotton (and preshrunk) fabrics; choose Permanent Press if the load consists of polyester or other synthetic

**Keep your colors bright** *by adding a non-chlorine bleach to the wash or by using a detergent boosted with color-safe bleach.*

**Air-drying clothes** *can save them from the wear and tear of tumbling in a dryer.*

fabrics; select the Low, Gentle, Delicate, or Air-Dry setting for fragile or sheer fabrics.

How long should you dry a load? If you have a full load of towels, choose the longest time—very dry. For most clothes, a normal setting will get clothes dry without overheating them. A few thick towels or blue jeans may still come out slightly damp, but it's safer to line-dry those the rest of the way than to risk overdrying the remaining items in the load.

If your load is a mix of fabrics, use the cycle and temperature (or the shortest drying time) that's recommended for the most delicate fabrics. When the dryer stops, remove the dry items; then restart the dryer to finish the load.

Do you need a fabric softener? Many people swear by these products, finding that they make clothes soft and fluffy, reduce wrinkles, prevent static cling, and make ironing easier. Others dismiss these claims as marketing hyperbole. If you do include fabric softeners in your wash-day routine, use the amount recommended; too much will make towels and similar items lose their absorbency.

# STAIN BUSTERS

---- ✳ ----

SMUDGES, DRIPS, DROPS, AND SMEARS—NO MATTER WHAT THEIR SOURCE, THE KEY TO KEEPING THEM FROM RUINING YOUR FAVORITE CLOTHES IS TO TAKE QUICK ACTION *BEFORE* THE STAIN GETS THE CHANCE TO DRY.

For most fabrics, this means blotting up the excess or rinsing the stain with cold water (don't rub; this spreads the stain and grinds it deeper), and then pretreating the spot. But thanks to modern detergents, keeping your favorite garments blemish-free is easier than ever.

When mixed with water, powdered detergents are especially effective at loosening ground-in dirt before washing so it can be carried away during the machine wash. Liquid detergents can help make oil, grease, and food stains disappear. Prewash stain removers (available as sprays, sticks, and liquids) are effective on most fibers.

Either chlorine or oxygen bleach ("color-safe") in the wash cycle can help your detergent remove tough stains, including rust spots and dye stains. But only chlorine bleach kills bacteria and viruses.

When pretreating, allow your stain-busting product to sit for a minute to a week, depending on the product. Save time by keeping a stain stick or spray near the hamper, and dabbing or spritzing it on blighted clothes. Put them in the hamper and forget about them; then wash as usual following the label directions. These stain busters usually eliminate all but the most stubborn spots.

**If all else fails, view your collection of stains as modern art.**

# COMMON STAINS AND
# HOW TO REMOVE THEM

---

IT'S MURPHY'S LAW: IF SOMETHING CAN SPILL, drip, ooze, or run, it will do so all over your lucky shirt or favorite dress. Fortunately, once you know how to treat these troublesome stains, you can save your beloved muumuu from ending up in the rag pile.

**Blood.** Rinse or presoak the garment in cold water and wash in cold water with laundry detergent. Do not use chlorine bleach, which can make the stain even worse.

**Chewing gum.** Rub the gummy spot with ice to harden it. Scrape away as much of the gum as possible with a dull knife. Saturate what remains with a prewash stain remover, rinse, and launder as usual.

**Chocolate.** Pretreat or prewash the garment in warm water with a cleaning product that contains enzymes. Launder as usual.

**Coffee.** Sponge with or soak in cold water. Apply a pretreating product on the stain. Wash as usual and air-dry; repeat if stain remains.

**Cosmetics.** Pretreat the spot with prewash stain remover or a liquid laundry detergent. Wash the garment in the water temperature recommended for the fabric.

**Crayon.** Scrape off surface wax with a dull knife. Soak the fabric in a product containing enzymes or oxygen bleach in the hottest water safe for the fabric. Launder using the hottest water it can withstand.

**Grass.** Presoak or prewash the garment in warm water in a bucket or your washing machine (using the presoak setting) with a detergent containing enzymes. Launder as usual with chlorine bleach if it's safe for the fabric. If the cleaning instructions advise against it, use oxygen bleach instead.

**Ink.** Place the stain over the mouth of a jar or glass. Hold the fabric taut. Drip rubbing alcohol through the stain so the ink will drop into the container as the soil is removed. Rinse thoroughly and launder as usual.

**Juice.** Soak in cold water, then apply a pretreating product on the stain. Launder as label instructions recommend. Air-dry; do not place in dryer until the stain is completely gone.

**Mildew.** Douse the garment with a diluted solution of bleach and launder as recommended for the garment. For mildewed leather, brush on an antiseptic mouthwash.

**Mud.** Brush off as much of the surface dirt as possible. Pretreat or presoak with a laundry detergent. Launder as usual.

**Perspiration, deodorants, antiperspirants.** Use a prewash stain remover; if the stains are old, apply white vinegar. Rinse, then launder using oxygen bleach in the hottest water that's safe to use with the fabric.

**Urine.** Cover with salt until all excess liquid is absorbed. Rinse in cold water. If a residual stain remains, apply white vinegar or hydrogen peroxide. Launder according to the instructions on the item's fabric-care label.

**Wine.** Generously sprinkle salt on the site of the stain to keep additional liquid from saturating the surface. Immerse item in cold water or a solution of borax for 30 minutes. Wash as label instructions recommend.

---

# TACKLING UNKNOWN STAINS

Wᴴᴬᵀ'ˢ ᵀᴴᴬᵀ ˢᴾᴼᵀ ᴼᴺ YOUR CHILD'S new white T-shirt? The remains of a chocolate ice-cream cone or the muddy aftermath of a skateboard stunt gone awry? If you don't know, try these easy remedies for combating mystery stains.

**Simple**    Wash the garment in detergent and the hottest water safe for the fabric and the suspected stain. If the stain doesn't disappear, try repeating the wash cycle until the spot fades away.

**Simpler**    Apply a prewash stain remover—available in sprays, liquids, and sticks—to the offending spot, then launder the garment in the hottest water that's safe for the fabric and for the stain.

**Simplest**    Track down the wearer of the garment. Query the guilty party as to the identity of the stain, and treat it with the best solution for the specific soil (see box at left).

## KNOW YOUR SPOT

If you don't know what the stain is, rinse or soak in cold water before treating. Get into the habit of checking wet clothes for stains before tossing them in the dryer, as this can permanently set the stain.

Unfortunately, you're not always near a washing machine or stain stick when a clothing disaster strikes. Not to worry: Some remedies will work even on set-in spots and stains. So treat the stain as soon as it is possible.

Pretreating works best on small spots and fresh stains. But for old stains and protein stains, presoaking is key. For fruit juice, coffee, and blood stains, use cold water (and do not use chlorine bleach, as it can make stains worse); otherwise fill a tub or sink with the warmest water safe for the fabric, add a healthy dose of detergent, and toss the garment in for at least

a half hour. Then wash with detergent and a nonchlorine bleach.

If, after all your efforts, a spot is still visible, defer to the expertise of your dry cleaner. Professional chemicals can often dissolve greases and oils that detergents available to consumers can't.

## Stain Patrol

Get the whole family in on the stain-busting game: Have your kids red-flag stains and spots by clipping a clothespin to a chocolate smudge or by tying grass-stained jeans in a loose knot before dumping them in the clothes hamper.

# STREAMLINING home
# Maintenance

---*---

**1** Schedule annual **inspections** for your home's roof and major systems, including the furnace and air conditioner. **2** Twice each year, venture into the **far corners** of your attic, basement, and garage to check for signs of water leakage. **3** At the start of each season, check the outside of your home for any **cracks** that have appeared. **4** Test smoke and carbon-monoxide detectors each month; **change batteries** yearly. **5** Clear walkways of leaves and any snow, ice, debris or algae that may make them **slippery.** **6** Assemble a kit of **essential tools** and store in a convenient place. **7** Learn to make minor **repairs** such as fixing a backed-up toilet, patching a hole in drywall, and recaulking a bathtub or shower. **8** **Insulate** older water heaters and leaky heat ducts to lower your energy bill. **9** Save energy in the **kitchen** by covering pots, opening the oven door sparingly, and using the microwave for reheating food. **10** Set the **thermostat** at 68°F (20°C) or lower in winter; 78°F (26°C) or higher in summer. ●

# MAINTENANCE AND REPAIR

**KEEPING YOUR HOUSEHOLD RUNNING SMOOTHLY**

\* —— \* —— \*

You know what they say about that ounce of prevention. If you ignore the advice and overlook home maintenance, the pound of cure can set you back hundreds, if not thousands, of dollars. Sooner or later, a neglected roof will leak. A furnace overworked from clogged air filters will need an expensive overhaul. And that leaky window will lead to dry rot in your house's framework and walls, necessitating a lot of expensive structural and esthetic repairs.

Prevention, in the form of maintenance tackled throughout the year, is the best way to keep these common household ills at bay. When little things do go wrong—as they inevitably will—knowing how to take care of them quickly means that you'll spend less of your valuable time waiting for those repair people to make an expensive appearance.

Most important, a well-maintained home is, by its very nature, safer and more comfortable and energy efficient.

# The Low-Maintenance Household

---

❋

---

THE FIRST STEP IN CREATING A LOW-MAINTENANCE HOME—ONE YOU DON'T NEED TO WORRY ABOUT WHEN RAINS FALL AND WINDS BLOW—IS TO SOLVE SMALL PROBLEMS BEFORE THEY NEED BIG, EXPENSIVE FIXES.

Some problems you can handle yourself, depending on how handy you are; others definitely call for a professional. In either case, if you're a homeowner, being aware of what requires regular maintenance—be it annually or on an as-needed basis—is the key to keeping your home running smoothly. Even if you live in an apartment or condominium, there are simple steps you can take to maintain your home in its best condition. The chart on page 82 can help you get started.

If you do bring in the pros for any jobs around your home, always keep a record of when the home repair was done and by whom (see the checklist on page 140). This information is important to have in case a problem should arise with any of the work that has been performed. It will also remind you of when you need to schedule your next maintenance check. In addition, it may be of help to prospective buyers (and your own realtor) if you should ever decide to sell your home.

---

## SIMPLE SOLUTIONS

## Making Your Home Run

A HOUSE MAY LAST FOR GENERATIONS, but its parts and systems won't last a lifetime without regular attention. A roof can spring a leak, for instance, or a furnace can fail on a frigid winter night. Here are three approaches to fixing what's wrong.

**Simple**
Fix it yourself. Even if you're mechanically challenged, try visiting a hardware store. You'll be surprised at how many easy-to-use remedies are available for common household ills.

**Simpler**
Let the professionals fix it. This solution works best for big-ticket jobs or a batch of smaller jobs that have accumulated over time. Be prepared: Help can be expensive and slow to arrive.

**Simplest**
Prevent problems in the first place by creating an annual maintenance plan (see page 82) and sticking to it. Regularly checking your home's major systems lets you head off emerging crises.

---

The simplest way to care for your home is through routine maintenance.

## ROOF PATROL

A sound roof is essential to the well-being of your home and everything in it. If your roof is flat enough to walk on safely and is not clad in a fragile material (such as tile or thin cedar shingles) you can perform simple maintenance tasks yourself with little more than a broom and a few basic tools. Such heights are inherently dangerous, so it goes without saying that you should be *very* careful up there.

Start with an inspection, which you should conduct before winter sets in. Don't wait until the first squall to make sure that roof gutters are clear of debris and that all roofing materials and flashing (those metal seams along the edges) are intact. Procrastination may result in an expensive and inconvenient fix later on.

Have someone help you haul the tools you'll need up the ladder and onto your roof. Using a broom, a lightweight leaf blower, or a hose with a spray attachment, remove leaves and dirt from the rooftop.

Next, use your (gloved) hands and a small brush to remove debris from gutters and downspouts. When all the visible debris is removed, pour water through the gutters and spouts to make sure they drain freely. If you prefer, you can clean gutters more safely (albeit more slowly) from a ladder held securely in place by an assistant.

Next, check the flashing around any chimneys, vents, skylights, or parapet walls. Look for gaps, cracks, and missing shingles. If you discover problems, be sure to call and make a service appointment now—before problems become emergencies.

## FIREPLACES AND STOVES

Newer fireplaces and stoves are better than traditional open hearths at controlling airflow and thus providing heat efficiently. But whatever the age of your fireplace or stove, a professional chimney inspection and cleaning each year is a must to keep soot and creosote from building up and leading to a chimney fire. If the fireplace

# PREVENTIVE MAINTENANCE

✳

THESE SIMPLE TASKS TAKE JUST a short amount of time to perform, but they are keys to preventing hazardous conditions and expensive repairs down the road. Below are the tasks you should be sure to tackle yourself during the year to keep your home running smoothly. If you pencil them in on your new calendar at the beginning of each year, you'll be more likely to remember to take care of them.

## OUTDOORS
*Take advantage of sunny days to inspect your home's exterior.*

| | Monthly | Seasonally | Semi-annually | Annually |
|---|:---:|:---:|:---:|:---:|
| **Clear your front walkway** surface of debris or algae. | ● | | | |
| **Check for surface cracks** in masonry and stucco; seal if needed. | | ● | | |
| **Scrub away mildew** on your home's exterior. | | | ● | |
| **Have chimney inspected;** clean if needed. | | | | ● |
| **Inspect and clean** roof, downspouts, gutters; repair if needed. | | | | ● |
| **Check seal of windows and doors;** weather-strip if needed. | | | | ● |

## INDOORS
*Grab a spare moment to complete these simple yet important tasks to ensure that your home is safe and well maintained.*

| | Monthly | Seasonally | Semi-annually | Annually |
|---|:---:|:---:|:---:|:---:|
| **Clean or change** furnace filters (monthly if you have pets). | | ● | | |
| **Have heating** and cooling systems professionally serviced. | | | | ● |
| **Test batteries** in smoke and carbon-monoxide detectors. | ● | | | |
| **Replace batteries** in smoke and carbon-monoxide detectors. | | | | ● |
| **Check washing machine and dishwasher** areas for leaks. | | ● | | |
| **Look for leaks** in the attic, basement, and garage. | | | ● | |
| **Inspect flooring** for wear; refinish, repair, or replace as needed. | | | | ● |
| **Check caulking** around tub, shower, sinks; replace as needed. | | | ● | |

or stove (woodburning or otherwise) is a major source of heat, have it inspected more frequently. Avoid burning resinous woods such as pine (which leave creosote in the flue) as well as evergreen boughs and large quantities of paper, which can flare up and quickly get out of control.

While you'll want to leave chimney cleaning to the pros, undertake minor maintenance yourself: If you burn wood, clean the stove or firebox between fires. Scoop up cool ashes and place them in a metal container. Close the flue or air intake after each use to keep indoor heat from escaping up the chimney.

## THE HEATING SYSTEM

On a cold night, your heating system is the last thing you want to have break down. Not only could such a mishap be uncomfortable and expensive, it could also be dangerous: A faulty gas or oil furnace may emit deadly carbon monoxide gas.

A fall tune-up for your furnace will prolong its life and keep your family safer while your home is closed up against the chill outdoors. Older forced-air furnaces should be serviced annually (every two years at the very least) to adjust the belts, lubricate the motor, check safety controls, adjust the air-fuel mixture, and inspect the combustion chamber for cracks that could admit carbon monoxide into your home. Furnaces that are less than 10 years old should be serviced every 3 to 5 years. You'll need a professional to check for leaks and to test the safety controls.

Depending on the type of heating system you have, there are things you can do yourself to keep it running smoothly and safely. If you have any electric baseboard heaters, the only maintenance required is regular vacuuming of dust.

For forced-air heating systems, clean or change the air filter once every heating season (more frequently if you have pets

*A cozy fire* can cause a structural blaze if creosote is allowed to build up in the flue and ignite. Have your chimney professionally inspected and cleaned once a year.

**Keep your walkways clear** *of moss, algae, and other growths that can become dangerously slippery when wet.*

them with caulk to keep air and water out of your walls. You'll want to check seldom-used places such as the attic, basement, and farthest corners of your garage for any sign of leaks. If you discover evidence of a water leak inside—such as wall or floor stains, streaks, or standing water—make appointments for needed repairs. A long-standing basement leak could be a symptom of poor grading or impeded drainage around the outside foundation—a serious problem that mere caulking can't solve.

At least twice a year, use a bleach solution to scrub clean any mildewed areas of your home's exterior. If unattended to, mildew will eat away your exterior paint, resulting in an expensive "fix-up" later.

As needed, sweep up and remove any debris from outdoor walkways and steps. If you notice any algae or other growths, scrub them off with a hard-bristled brush and bleach. Pedestrian surfaces covered with algae, moss, or other substances can be slippery and dangerous when wet.

or your house tends to collect dust) and keep the surrounding area clean. Move combustible materials well away from the furnace. Review the manual for your heating system: Some systems require more maintenance than others.

Even well-maintained furnaces and appliances can emit toxic carbon monoxide (which is both odorless and colorless), making carbon-monoxide detectors essential. Test detectors monthly, and replace the batteries once a year.

## LEAKS AND MILDEW

Spot-check your home's exterior and interior once each season. If you see any cracks in masonry or stucco, between siding and window or door frames, or in corners, seal

### Book Ahead

Don't wait until your home's furnace, air conditioner, chimney, or roof needs immediate attention before you call for service. Instead, save money by scheduling visits a month ahead of the time when these items see heaviest use—and repair people are in greatest demand.

Indoors, regularly peek beneath your dish-washer and washing machine and at the pipes that serve them. Many of the larger appliances have removable panels along the floor, which allow you to peer under-neath. Such sleuthing will reveal small leaks that can sometimes go undetected for months. Also check for leaks under the sink, especially where the dishwasher drain hooks up to the main drain.

If you spot a leak, you may be able to fix it yourself. Simply tighten the nuts on the pipe joints that service the dishwasher and the sink. If you can't stop the flow of water yourself, call a plumber.

## WHY WEATHER-STRIP?

In many homes during cold weather, warm indoor air escapes outside through numer-ous little holes and gaps surrounding pipes and vents; along seams between walls and floors; and between masonry and siding materials. Wind gusts can also force cold air through these openings and into your house, raising your heating bill. As your house ages and settles, or expands and con-tracts from changes in temperature or humidity, these gaps can open and admit moisture into your walls. If you see light around your doors and windows from inside or feel a draft, it's time to seal with weather stripping or caulk.

Weather stripping—a narrow piece of metal, vinyl, rubber, felt, or foam that seals the space between the door and the frame—can be installed on the interior of windows and doors. Installation of most weather stripping is simple, involv-ing either stick-on materials or the more durable metal stripping that is put on with small tacks. Experts recommend weather-stripping the entire perimeter of exterior doors: Affix one continuous strip along the top and sides and attach a floor "sweep" to the inside bottom of the door. Most weather-stripping kits and door sweeps come with detailed instructions.

If you find gaps on outsides of window or door frames, they'll need to be caulked. You can do this simply, by using a caulk-ing gun with an inexpensive, exterior-rated caulk. Latex caulk is simplest to use: The excess can be cleaned up with water. It can also be painted. Begin by cleaning the area thoroughly to give the caulk a good surface to adhere to. Simply squeeze the gun trig-ger and apply the caulk. Smooth the caulk line and clean the excess with a wet sponge before the caulk dries.

**Sealing your home's exterior** *against the elements will help prevent expensive damage to the framework inside.*

# BUILDING A BASIC TOOL KIT

---❋---

YOU REALLY CAN HANDLE MANY MINOR REPAIRS AND HOME-IMPROVEMENT PROJECTS AROUND YOUR HOME ALL BY YOURSELF—AND YOU DON'T NEED A GARAGE FULL OF SUPERCHARGED TOOLS TO GET THE JOB DONE RIGHT.

You'll need a standard claw hammer; an adjustable wrench; a tape measure; several sizes of screwdrivers (both standard and Phillips head); a cordless drill and set of bits; and standard slip-joint, needle-nose, and wire-cutting pliers.

You'll also want a hacksaw for cutting metals and plastics; a medium-size pair of tongue-and-groove pliers; a pair of locking pliers; a general-purpose wood saw; a putty knife; a utility knife; a square; a small level; a utility light and several long, heavy-duty extension cords; a dependable flashlight; a battery-operated stud finder; and a plunger for minor plumbing fixes.

Your essential tools will come in handy for routine repairs such as stopping leaks at the base of a faucet (with your adjustable wrench) or for hanging shelves or pictures (with your hammer, drill, stud finder, tape measure, and level). Needle-nose pliers are just the thing for reaching into tight spaces, twisting small wires, and holding small metal parts and nails in place for screwing or hammering. Other tools for occasional projects: an electric saber saw, a set of socket wrenches, a circular saw, an electric palm or orbital sander, an assortment of paintbrushes, and a staple gun.

Finally, stock an assortment of nuts, bolts, screws, and metal washers; rubber washers for leaky faucets; duct tape; several sizes of nails or tacks; fine sandpaper; lubricating oil for door hinges; a versatile glue; and a container of liquid drain opener. (For an expanded tool list, see page 138.)

When maintenance emergencies come up, you'll save time
and money if you already have the tools you need.

# KEEPING TOOLS HANDY

※

**W**HAT COULD BE MORE REWARDING than doing it yourself? With the right tools, you can make many common repairs around your home—even if you've never taken a shop class in your life. Getting everything together in a convenient place is the first step toward simplifying home maintenance.

**For on-the-move repairs,** *stash essentials in a wide-mouthed carpenter's bag designed specifically for toting tools.*

**Store extra** *screws and bolts in jars where they're easy to see. Secure lids to undersides of shelves so you can open jars with one hand.*

**Keep your workshop neat** *by mounting tools on a pegboard and drawing outlines of items to show where they go.*

**Short on space?** *Then keep essential tools in a roll-up canvas bag. It's easy to stash in a hall closet or kitchen drawer, where it's always ready for quick fixes that are needed around the house.*

# WHEN THINGS GO WRONG

---✳---

Fixing things yourself has two big advantages: You save time and you save money. After all, who has the leisure—or the inclination—to wait all day for an expensive repair person to stop by?

Of course, you probably shouldn't attempt to rewire your house or retile your bathroom floor without training, but you can simplify your life by learning to do some of the essential repairs on your own.

What common problems will you be able to solve yourself? Clearing a backed-up toilet is perhaps the most urgent repair, followed by patching small holes in drywall or plaster and recaulking a bathtub. There are also some elementary household repairs that you can easily tackle with the help of common household items. Here are a few simple but important fixes you can take care of yourself.

## BACKED-UP TOILETS

When the toilet water threatens to overflow or the kitchen or bathroom sink regurgitates, your natural inclination is probably to get as far away as possible from the germs and gunk within and to reach for the phone. You'll probably get a busy signal—there's a reason plumbers are the busiest repair people around. Be brave: You can fix the problem yourself, often in a few simple steps.

Consider the case where the water in your toilet bowl continues to rise above its normal level after you flush. This is not a pretty picture, but if you've got kids who have recently discovered the won-

ders of toilet paper, it may well be a familiar one. The first move to keep a bad situation from getting worse is to remove the top of the tank and flip the rubber stopper in the bottom of the tank back over the drain hole. This will stop the flow of water into the bowl.

Next, place the plunger cup snugly over the bowl's drain opening and give it a few vigorous pumps. The idea is to force the obstruction beyond a U-shaped section of toilet pipe, called the "trap," and into the straighter (and wider) drainpipe. The blockage should then flow away, and take with it any backed-up water.

**You can fix some backups yourself.**

If your efforts are of no avail, the problem may lie elsewhere in the drainage system. Now that you've ruled out a simple clog, it's time to call your busy plumber. Meanwhile, don't pour caustic liquid plumbing products into the bowl. That way, the plumber doesn't have to deal with harsh chemicals when making the repair.

the blockage—or if you've noticed that several of your home's other sinks are also draining sluggishly—the problem is likely to be deep inside your main house drain and well out of your reach. Once again, you'll need that plumber.

If your garbage disposal stops working, the good news is that most disposals

**When sinks in the kitchen or bathroom back up, pouring liberal doses of very hot water down the drain will often melt clogs away.**

One way to prevent such mishaps is to make clear to your family (children especially) that human waste and toilet paper are the only things allowed in the bowl. Keep a small wastebasket near the toilet for disposal of all other items.

### STOPPED-UP SINKS

When sinks in the kitchen or bathroom back up, pouring liberal doses of very hot water down the drain will often help by melting greasy clogs away. If that doesn't work, place your handy plunger over the drain opening, and perform three or four swift pumps; then pause to see if the sink drains. If it doesn't, try again. As a last resort before calling that busy plumber, try using liquid drain opener.

On tub and bathroom sink drains, you need to cover the overflow valve near the rim. As you gently push the plunger down, hold a slightly damp cloth over the overflow valve. Alternatively, pour in some of that liquid drain opener into the primary drain and cross your fingers.

If the drain opener or several short sessions with the plunger won't dislodge

have a built-in reset button. Heavy loads will sometimes cause the motor to overheat; after switching off the disposal and waiting a minute or two, you can press the reset button (usually red) near the bottom of the unit; then restart the disposal. Normally, if a disposal refuses to turn on—unless the drain is obviously filled up with garbage—this reset button is the quickest way to get it running again.

## Plumbing With Petroleum Jelly

A backed-up toilet is troubling, but usually, with a little effort, you can have it cleared and flushing again soon. Apply a thin ring of petroleum jelly around the rim of the rubber plunger cup. Doing this provides for a tighter seal against the bowl—and improves the effectiveness of the pumping action.

If this doesn't work, shut off the power to the disposal unit by either unplugging it or turning off the circuit breaker if the unit is hardwired. Use the wrench that comes with the disposal to turn the mechanism and make sure it's not jammed (the wrench usually fits in a hexagonal recess in the bottom of the disposal). If it won't budge, shine a flashlight down into the disposal to see if you can determine the cause of the jam. If you don't find anything amiss there, or you just see a lot of water, then insert the handle of a broom or plunger into the drain and move the handle back

from entering the drain. You can also buy inexpensive plastic drain screens that can be placed over bathroom sink drains, right over the built-in stoppers. These screens will catch and hold hair, soap slivers, and other potential drain cloggers and make it easy for you to lift out the obstructions and toss them in the trash before they cause costly plumbing backups.

Rather than relying on expensive and usually toxic drain openers, every month or so sprinkle about ¼ cup (60ml) of baking soda into your sink and tub drains, followed with just enough warm water to

**To make faucet washers last longer, turn the faucet off but don't tighten the handle more than is needed to stop the water.**

and forth. This should dislodge the blade, which may be wedged against a piece of silverware, a bottle cap, or some other small item that has fallen in unnoticed. Use long kitchen tongs—never use your fingers—to pull the culprit out.

### PREVENTIVE PLUMBING

Here are a few ways to keep the plumber away and your fix-it jobs to a minimum:

Never pour cooking grease into drains —it stops them up as it cools and hardens. Instead, chill it in an empty milk or juice carton in the refrigerator and dispose of it in the regular garbage.

Use inexpensive drain screens, available in hardware and grocery stores (they are made of either plastic or metal), in the kitchen sink, the bathtub, and the shower to prevent food particles, hair, or small items like jewelry and toothpaste caps

get the powder well into the drain. Then pour in 1 cup (240ml) of white vinegar. Let the clumpy mixture stand a few hours or overnight to dissolve scum and bacteria buildup in the pipe bends beneath the sink or tub drains, then flush the drain with hot water. Following this procedure regularly will keep your drains working freely without harming any of your plumbing fixtures or the environment.

To make faucet washers last longer and to prevent leaks, turn the faucet off but don't tighten the handle any more than is needed to stop the water. Cranking handles forcefully into the off position wears down the washers faster.

To make washing machines operate better and last longer, install inexpensive hose screens on the hot and cold water hoses to keep sediment from clogging the washing machine's pumps and valves.

Check the screens at least once or twice a year and replace them both if they are full of sediment or debris.

## CORRECTIVE CAULKING

Dingy, cracked, or mildewed bathtub or shower caulk can make even a sparkling clean bathroom appear dirty and unappealing. If you've resisted replacing the caulk because it seemed like a big job, hesitate no more. You can make this simple repair, which packs a big decorative punch, with very little effort and only minimal amount of experience.

One of the common mistakes many people make when they notice that the caulking around a tub or shower stall has become stained or mildewed (or that some has fallen out) is simply to spread a fresh layer of caulk over the dingy or crumbling area. It does brighten the bathroom—for a week or two. Then the underlying mildew eats its way up through the new layer of caulk, treating the recent arrival as a little snack. Before long, you find that you (and your bathroom) are back to dingy and crumbling square one.

However, even the mechanically challenged can usually recaulk the right way by following a few simple steps:

Using a stiff putty knife and a small, inexpensive razor scraper, remove all old caulking material around the tub. Dig out as much old caulk as possible so that a shallow groove is formed along the entire edge between the bathtub and the tile or the tub or shower surround.

Next, thoroughly scrub the entire area with a bleach-based cleaner and a stiff

**The caulking** *around a shower or tub can become mildewed if you fail to keep it dry. If that happens, you'll need to recaulk.*

brush. Rinse well, and allow to dry completely. A fan temporarily directed at the area will speed the drying process.

Using a latex-based tub-and-tile caulk, in either a squeeze tube or a caulking gun, fill the shallow groove with a thin, continuous bead of caulk. While the line of caulk is still fresh and before a skin starts to set and harden—within a few minutes, at most—moisten your fingertip and use it to smooth the caulk out and push it thoroughly into any gaps.

Then carefully wipe any excess caulk with a damp cloth. The trick is to use the least amount of caulk necessary to fill the small gap between two different materials and surfaces. It should be nearly invisible when complete, and not protrude any farther than the tile or the edge of the tub or shower. Otherwise, it can act as a trap for moisture and allow mildew to grow. Let the caulk set for as long as the package directions indicate (it's usually overnight). Finally, you can probably avoid ever having to do this job again by regularly drying tub surfaces, shower walls, fixtures, and caulked areas with a clean towel. If stains do appear, try cleaning the caulking with a mildew-killer or other commercially available grout-and-caulk cleaner.

### ON THE WALL

If you've recently rearranged the family portraits on the living room wall or reorganized the shelving in your home office, chances are you have a wall or two that is less than picture-perfect. Yes, you could always just hang something over the holes to hide them from sight, but you can patch small holes in drywall or plaster them almost as easily by yourself. Here's how:

Grab your vacuum and suck away any loose plaster, paint chips, or dust from the hole. Using a putty knife, fill the hole with a premixed spackling compound (readily found in hardware stores) and smooth it level with the surface of the wall. Let the compound dry thoroughly—a few hours or overnight. Then smooth it with a damp sponge and paint over the spackled area to match the color of your wall.

If the hole is deep, the spackling compound will shrink slightly when dry, and a second application may be needed to make the hole smooth and even with the rest of the wall surface.

A shortcut: If you have leftover latex paint that matches the wall, add a small amount of paint to the premixed spackling compound and use a putty knife to fill the hole with the paint-and-spackling mixture. If done carefully, the patch may blend in well enough to require no further sanding or painting. This works only for

---

**SIMPLE SOLUTIONS**

## PLUGGING WALL HOLES

I F YOU JUST MOVED THAT LOVELY VAN GOGH print to a more prominent place for your party tonight—only to be faced with unsightly holes where it once hung—you can have a presentable surface before the guests arrive:

**Simple**

Squeeze spackling compound (for plaster walls) or wood putty into the holes, smooth with a putty knife, and wipe away any remaining traces of putty with a damp sponge.

**Simpler**

Fill the holes with white toothpaste and wipe the edges of the holes clean. The texture and consistency of toothpaste hold up nicely for a temporary fix in plaster walls.

**Simplest**

If you don't have time to fix it, hide it! Hang another print or artwork in the now-vacant Van Gogh wall space. Or dim the lights, and guests will never know about the holes.

small holes, such as those caused by picture hooks. A larger, deeper perforation may require two applications of the spackling compound; sand after each application has dried and touch up with paint.

## QUICK FIXES

A loose screw in a door hinge (or any wood material) can be tightened by removing the screw, inserting a few common wood toothpicks or matchsticks, breaking them off at surface level, and then replacing the screw. Double-hung windows that don't move up and down freely can be lubricated by rubbing a dry bar of paraffin in the tracks on the sides of the windows. This also works for wooden dresser drawers or for doors that rub against their frames. The tip of a common graphite pencil can be rubbed on metal door latches to make them close more smoothly without banging on the latch plate in the door frame.

Among the most useful items to have handy for quick fixes are a wide roll of masking tape and another roll of common vinyl duct tape. You can write on masking tape with a felt marker and make temporary "Wet Paint" signs. A tear in a vinyl chair seat or car seat can be patched with heavy-duty duct tape.

A broken cup handle can be reattached with epoxy, polyvinyl chloride, or another strong glue meant for porous surfaces. You can hold it in the proper position with a piece of masking tape while the glue dries. (Avoid putting these glued items in the dishwasher; hot water may melt the seals.) Cracked window glass can be temporarily held in place with strips of duct tape.

## SIMPLY PUT...

### GLUE TALK

**epoxy** • Used to bond dissimilar surfaces, such as glass to wood, or plastic to metal. It's waterproof, rigid, and very strong.

**polyvinyl acetate** • Fancy name for the old familiar white glue in a squeeze bottle. It dries clear and strong, and is good for interior use on wood, paper, and ceramics.

**polyvinyl chloride** • This is just the glue for broken china. Also adheres to marble, wood, or metal.

Wrapping a thickness or two of masking tape around the end of a loose chair rung and then tapping it back into its hole can provide a temporary fix. Wrapping a thickness of vinyl duct tape around any tool's smooth metal handle can make for a better grip. All manner of things that break into pieces or come apart can be temporarily taped back together with duct tape until permanent repairs or replacements can be made—a cracked broom handle, cardboard storage boxes, exposed metal edges, eyeglasses, even a loose doorknob.

When working with something that has small parts, roll a piece of masking tape into a loop (sticky side out), and flatten it against your work surface. Press the small items onto the tape to prevent them from rolling onto the floor and getting lost while you're in the midst of a repair.

# ENERGY-SAVING TIPS

---- ✳ ----

O F COURSE, YOU WANT YOUR HOME TO BE WARM AND COZY DURING THE
WINTER MONTHS, AND COOL AND COMFORTABLE DURING THE DOG DAYS
OF SUMMER. BUT YOU ALSO WANT TO KEEP YOUR ENERGY BILLS UNDER CONTROL.

Energy-smart day-to-day living is easier than you might think. Save cold cash year round with these simple steps.

## HEATING AND COOLING

If your home's heating or cooling unit is more than 15 years old, you might want to replace it with one of today's energy-efficient models. The newer models, which are better insulated and have motors that require less maintenance, pay for themselves in energy savings, frequently in as little as three to five years.

If you're not ready to make such a large purchase right now, you can wrap

insulation around heating ducts. But first check your ductwork for dirt streaks, especially near the seams. A streak indicates an air leak, which needs to be sealed with metal-backed duct tape before you add the insulating jacket. If the furnace ductwork appears to have been insulated and you think it might contain asbestos, make sure you have a professional test it before you begin. If asbestos is present, have it wrapped with duct-pipe insulation to protect you and your family.

A sure way to save on winter heating bills is to open the drapes during the day and let the sun shine in, and to draw them at night to keep the heat from radiating out. Set the thermostat at 68°F (20°C) or lower during the day, and set it at 55°F (13°C) at night or when you're away. For every degree you lower your thermostat, you'll save 3 to 5 percent on your monthly heating bill. Also consider installing a thermostat with a built-in timer. While you can easily adjust your thermostat yourself to comfortable temperatures, it's more efficient to have a system that does it for you automatically.

To keep your home cool in summer, draw the drapes and close the windows to keep hot air and the sun's burning rays out. Set the thermostat at 78°F (26°C) or higher when you're home.

## Morning Warm-Ups

If you awake to a chilly home, resist the urge to push the thermostat to 90°F (32°C). It won't warm things up more quickly—it will make your heating system burn longer and use more energy. Set it instead at an agreeable 68°F (20°C) and sip a hot beverage while you wait for the house to warm up. The reward for your patience will be lower utility bills.

Don't place your air-conditioning thermo-stat near lamps, appliances, or in direct sunlight. Heat in these areas is sensed by the thermostat and could cause the air conditioner to run longer than necessary.

## LIGHTENING UP

Since energy for lighting accounts for some 10 percent of your electric bill, you can save by lightening up on your wattage. If you're using 100-watt bulbs where 60-watt bulbs would do, consider replacing them. Or switch to fluorescent bulbs that screw into standard sockets. The newer ones give off a warmer light that's closer to the light of incandescent bulbs.

Lighten up on your interior decorating, too: Pale colors for walls, draperies, rugs, and upholstery reflect light and can reduce the number of lamps needed to adequately light a room.

Outdoors, replace incandescent lighting with high-pressure sodium or outdoor fluorescent bulbs for additional savings. Or try solar-powered pathway lamps (with batteries that store photovoltaic energy for nighttime use) or high-efficiency sodium lamps for security lighting.

## COOKING UP SAVINGS

It's quite easy to cook up energy savings in the kitchen. If you keep range-top burners and reflectors clean, they'll reflect the heat better and require less energy for cooking. If you cook with electricity, turn off the burners several minutes before the end of the allotted cooking time. The burners will stay hot long enough to finish the job without using any more electricity.

When you have a choice between using the range top and the oven, go with the former to save energy. If you do use the oven, open it sparingly; each time you open it, heat escapes and the oven will use even more energy to maintain the temperature.

Use a pressure cooker and a microwave oven whenever possible; both save energy. When you're boiling water, keep a lid on the pot; water boils faster when you use a top to hold in the heat.

## Safe and Warm

The traditional home hot-water setting of 140°F (60°C) can scald skin—a particular danger if there are young children in your household. So what's the solution? Turn down the thermostat on your water heater to ensure that the mercury doesn't top the now-suggested 120°F (49°C). Your family members will bathe more safely and your energy bill will be lower.

# STEPS to a
# Safer HOME

——※——

**1** Buy or assemble a **first-aid kit** and keep it where you can
grab it quickly. **2** Install smoke and carbon-monoxide **detec-**
**tors;** keep fire extinguishers within easy reach in the kitchen and
garage. **3** **Check** your home for radon gas, crumbling asbestos,
and lead paint. **4** Lock away all ladders, garden tools, trash cans,
patio furniture, and other outdoor accessories that could help a
**burglar** break and enter. **5** Burglarproof **entry points** with
window locks, dead bolts, and security devices for sliding glass doors.
**6** Stash your spare **house key** in a creative place—not under
the doormat or beneath a flowerpot. **7** Engrave **ID numbers**
on cameras and other valuables; photograph these items in case of theft
or fire. **8** Consider installing a professionally monitored **alarm**
system. It's costly but secure. **9** Create a family **survival kit**
with enough food, water, and other essentials to last 72 hours after a
major disaster. **10** Be prepared for the fury of Mother Nature.
Secure your home against natural **disasters. ●**

# SAFE AT HOME

## SIMPLIFYING HOUSEHOLD SAFETY AND SECURITY

\* —— \* —— \*

Your home is your family's safe haven. It's the place you return to each evening, leaving your workday worries—and the outside world—behind once you secure the front door. While your walls provide a safe refuge within which you can weather the storms of daily life, ensuring your family's physical safety while inside requires some extra precautions. These include creating a first-aid and disaster-survival kit, installing detectors to alert you to fire and other hazards, securing doors and windows against thieves, and battening down the hatches in anticipation of Mother Nature's fury.

These simple security measures will prepare your family, your neighborhood, and your home for whatever big and little surprises life and nature happen to throw your way. If you make the effort to fortify your household's security and your family's safety, you'll sleep much better at night knowing that home, sweet home is also home, *safe* home.

# THE SAFETY ESSENTIALS

---*---

YOU DON'T NEED TO SPEND A BUNDLE TO KEEP YOUR HOME SAFE FROM ENVIRONMENTAL AND MAN-MADE HAZARDS. ALL IT TAKES IS KNOWLEDGE OF WHAT CAN GO WRONG, AND A FEW SIMPLE STEPS TO PREPARE YOURSELF.

Being prepared to act when an accident or a fire occurs and having the necessary detectors in good working order to give you warning will help you rest easier. (For an overview of what to have on hand, see the list on page 132.)

## FIRST AID

Because accidents happen, you'll want to be prepared to treat scrapes, burns, bites, and other minor and major mishaps that may occur at home. A prepackaged first-aid kit is the simplest solution; these come stocked with all the bandages, tools, and antiseptic wipes you may need.

But it might be less expensive to create your own kit. Make sure you have the following essentials in your medicine chest: adhesive bandage strips, gauze pads, sterile cotton balls, antiseptic wipes (or an antiseptic solution), a chemical-activated instant cold pack, eyewash, blunt-tipped

## FIRE AND SMOKE

Because the toxic gases from a fire could keep you from waking up should a fire ignite while you're sleeping, maintaining working smoke detectors for every level of your home is a must. Install detectors on the ceiling (smoke rises) in every bedroom and outside bedroom doors, at the top of stairways, and in any den or office in the basement. Test the devices monthly and replace the batteries at least once a year.

Fire extinguishers should also be kept on each floor as well as in every bedroom and in any room where a fire could occur, such as the kitchen or a workshop. Check fire extinguishers monthly—it could keep a small mishap from becoming a disaster.

Another safety must-have is a carbon-monoxide detector. This deadly, colorless, odorless gas is becoming a threat in more and more of today's energy-efficient and airtight homes. The source of carbon

**Because the toxic gases from a fire can actually keep you from waking up at night, smoke detectors are a must.**

scissors, tweezers, a thermometer, cotton swabs, and activated charcoal and syrup of ipecac in case of poisoning. And be sure to keep the phone numbers of your nearest poison-control center, your pharmacy, and family members' doctors by the telephone.

monoxide is usually faulty burning in, or poor venting of, a furnace or another appliance. Your first defense is to maintain these items properly. Carbon-monoxide detectors, which resemble smoke alarms, are an essential backup.

## ASBESTOS AND LEAD

If your home was built before 1978, it may contain asbestos around furnaces, pipes, heat ducts, and boilers; in the adhesive and backing beneath your linoleum floor; and in "cottage-cheese" ceilings. The dust of this carcinogen can cause serious lung ailments when inhaled.

If the asbestos is in your garage near the furnace and you rarely go there, you should simply be aware of it and regularly check its condition. Asbestos generally is not a problem unless it's disturbed (by a leak in the roof or a child's bouncing ball, for example). If it's crumbling or otherwise in poor condition, hire a licensed contractor experienced in asbestos removal to seal it, repair it, or get it out of your home; look under "Asbestos" in the Yellow Pages.

Lead paint, which is commonly found in homes that were built before 1980, has also made today's environmental dishonor roll. Lead-tainted dust can escape during cleaning, and if enough of this substance is ingested or inhaled, it can cause permanent brain damage and other serious harm, especially to children, mothers-to-be, and older adults. If you live in an older home, you might want to hire a trained professional to conduct a hazard assessment.

To check for lead yourself, chip off a bit of suspect paint—right down to the bare wood—and then either send it to a laboratory for analysis or buy an inexpensive test kit at a hardware store. If you do find lead, cover the area with wallpaper, paneling, or new lead-free paint, and frequently wash children's hands and faces as well as toys and pacifiers to reduce their exposure to dust containing lead. Once tainted surfaces are covered, they are usually considered safe unless they chip or peel.

## RADON GAS

The second leading cause of lung cancer, radioactive radon gas is a serious environmental threat in many parts of the world. Typically, this odorless element moves up through the soil and seeps into buildings through cracks and pores in the foundation and through gaps in floors. Trapped inside, it can build to dangerous levels. If a test kit (available at hardware stores) indicates radon is present, hire a certified radon professional to prevent infiltration.

## Fire Extinguisher Checkup

Is that extinguisher hanging on your kitchen wall still ready to protect you from a fire? Check both the pressure gauge and the date tag. If the pressure is low or the date is more than a year old, have the extinguisher serviced by licensed personnel recommended by the local fire department. Otherwise, as long as the pin is intact, you're ready to aim should the need arise.

# Securing Your Home Against Intruders

───── ✳ ─────

Whether your home is humble or palatial, there's probably something inside it of interest to thieves. But most burglars aren't angling to fill their bags with Grandma's china or your best crystal.

Instead, they're after common items—the television, a radio, a CD player, a nifty pair of sneakers—that can be sold quickly and easily down the street.

Most burglars are not exceedingly skilled at their game. The majority are teens or young adults on the prowl for an obviously unoccupied, unsecured home. Few have high-tech lock-picking devices; their tools are usually as simple as their methods—they'll pry open a sliding glass door with a screwdriver, or stand on a patio chair or shimmy up a drainpipe to reach an unlocked window.

The good news is that your antitheft strategies can be simple, too. A few basic precautions will usually keep all but the most determined burglars from giving your home a second glance. One of the simplest and most effective ways to deter burglars from breaking into your apartment building, condominium complex, or house is to get to know your neighbors. Become involved in—or create—a neighborhood watch program. These programs, generally created with the help of the local police department, have proved to be effective in reducing criminal activity while bringing communities closer together.

In addition to meeting your neighbors, if you join a watch group you'll learn about any suspicious activities, crimes, or acts of

Burglars look for an easy target;
make your home a hard one.

vandalism that have recently been reported in your neighborhood—and how you can help prevent more from happening.

## ALL IN A DAY'S WORK

You probably worry most about intruders at night, but more than half of all break-ins actually occur in the daytime. Today's dual-career couples, with their often-empty homes, have made weekday mornings the prime time for burglaries. If you live in a condominium complex or in an apartment building, many of the exterior safety measures may already be in place.

A gated community or a locked apartment building entrance will discourage an intruder. If your building or community is not secured in such a way or is open around the clock, contact your landlord to discuss installing a lock; or put security on the agenda at the next meeting of your home-owners' association.

If yours is a detached home, the first step toward a safer home is to take a walk around its perimeter. Is the vegetation near your doors and windows well trimmed? Thick shrubbery provides a perfect cover for intruders, allowing them to work un-detected by your neighbors. Make a note to prune any overgrown greenery the next time you're working in the garden.

Then look around your yard. Do you have ladders, sturdy trash cans, stackable boxes, garden tools, or patio furniture that could help a thief break in? If so, resolve to stow them in your garage or toolshed. Even a metal drainpipe can provide access to second-story windows, which are often left unlocked. Stop climbers in their tracks

**A home that looks occupied** *is a less invit-ing target for burglars. Lights turned on by timers can help convey that impression.*

by spreading a bit of petroleum jelly along pipes that reach ground level. You needn't go much higher than the first floor, so a small stepladder, a big tub of jelly, and some disposable rubber gloves are all you'll need. Reapply whenever the pipe loses its slick.

## WINDOWS AND DOORS

Next, check all your windows. Those at street level are favorite entry points because they're easily reachable and often hidden from view. Make a note to install grilles, bars, or metal security grates that open from the inside with a safety latch to give your family an exit in case of fire. It's best to get a locksmith or gate manufacturer to install the device rather than doing it yourself.

First- and second-story windows can be secured simply by adding a pickproof locking device—such as a keyed lock, a sash lock, or a locking bolt, depending on

**An iron grille** *is an effective barrier against intruders, but it can also trap people inside in a fire unless it has a safety latch.*

or eyebolts into the holes with enough of the heads exposed so you can remove them quickly when you need to open the window. Be aware, however, that one window in every bedroom has to be entirely free of all these devices so that occupants and rescuers can easily see how to open the window in case there is a fire.

When you leave the house, place valuables where passers-by can't see them, or close the drapes or blinds. Always lock up whenever you leave, of course, and keep doors locked while you're in your home. Doors leading outside are where more than three-quarters of all burglars gain entry, and where your efforts are most likely to have a dramatic impact on your family's safety and your home's security.

Sliding glass doors are the type most vulnerable to break-ins, as their rudimentary locks are easy to pick. The simplest

the type of window you have. For sash windows, purchase a simple gadget that screws onto the inside of the frame at the height you choose and contains a knob you can slide out (to prevent the window from opening past the chosen height) or slide in (to allow free opening). If your home has sliding aluminum-frame windows, an aluminum traveler, fastened by a hand-tightened bolt or knob you secure along the lower window track at a desired distance from the opening edge, will keep intruders from sliding open the window should they defeat the primary lock.

You can also create your own pin lock by drilling a hole through the top of the inside sashes and three-quarters of the way through the outside sash at a slight downward angle. Slide narrower-diameter nails

**Sliding glass doors are the type most vulnerable to break-ins, as their rudimentary locks are easy to pick.**

solution is a metal bar or a length of wood dowelling (a section of broom handle also works) placed in the lower door track. Determined thieves have, however, been known to circumvent these by lifting the glass panels out of their tracks. Make it harder for them by adding a pin lock. You can buy one from your local locksmith or at your neighborhood hardware store. Or, as with windows, do it yourself with a drill and nails. You can remove the nail from the inside, but a burglar won't be able to without breaking the glass. As an added security measure, cover the glass with a polycarbonate glazing.

Take a close look at your front door—nearly a third of all burglars gain entrance here. Your door should be made of either solid wood—at least 1³/₈ inches (3.5cm) thick—or steel. Replace any thin, hollow doors, which are a snap for a determined thief to kick open. Whatever type of door it is, the hinges should not be on the outside, as the pins could easily be removed and the entire door taken off its frame. If the door has exterior hinges, replace them with hinges whose pins can't be removed.

## LOCKS AND KEYS

Make sure the lock is equally solid: As a rule, a dead bolt should have a 1-inch (2.5cm) throw bolt and an interlocking frame. And yes, your door needs a dead bolt *in addition* to the keyed knob set. Don't use a dual-cylinder lock—the kind with a key for both sides: This can trap you in the house in case of emergency. If you have one now, replace it. You may also want to install dead-bolt locks on the door from the garage into your home.

If your door has a window or a glass panel, secure it with a decorative grille that has nonremovable screws, or install over the glass a break-resistant plastic panel. If a window lies within an arm's length of the door, make sure that the door's dead bolt is out of reach should an intruder break the glass in the window and reach inside. Cover the window with a curtain or shade to keep prying eyes out.

Can you detect who's knocking before you open the front door? If you don't already have a peephole, hire a locksmith to install one in your door when he or she comes to install your new dead bolt.

A simpler—and much less expensive—approach is to buy a peephole and install it yourself. Choose the type with a fish-eye lens; its wide-angle view will allow you to see almost everything—and everyone—on your doorstep before you unlock that dead bolt and open the door. Make sure your porch light is at least 40 watts to properly illuminate nighttime visitors.

Secure gate latches and garage and shed doors with sturdy padlocks that are designed to resist prowlers and stand up to rain and freezing temperatures.

# SIMPLY PUT...

### LOCK TALK

**single-cylinder dead-bolt lock** • Opened with a key on the outside and a thumb turn on the inside.

**dual-cylinder lock** • A bolt lock that has a key for both inside and outside. Replace it with a single-cylinder lock, which is safer.

**privacy lock** • A commonly used interior lock that has a push button or thumb turn on the inside, with a hole on the outside that allows someone to open the door with either a special key or a straightened paper clip in case there is an emergency.

## Lights, Sound, Action

You're out for the evening. How do you manage to keep that bit of information under wraps? Set timers so that the lights go off in various rooms at appropriate times, and don't forget to hook up radios or TVs. The sound of someone seemingly chattering away inside will discourage most prowlers from trying to get in.

Now, consider your "oops" key. Does the spare that lets you in when you've lost your house keys sit beneath the doormat, in the mailbox, or underneath the potted plant next to the door? These are the first places thieves look for keys in hopes of easy access to your home. Move the spare to a different, more creative location.

## 24-HOUR SECURITY

Although most burglaries occur during the day, motion-sensor lights, affixed well out of reach in your yard and around the perimeter of your home, may discourage a nighttime prowler. And keep your outside porch light on all night. Lights are your least expensive insurance policy against theft, since the last thing a burglar wants is to be seen. Whenever you'll be gone for more than a few hours, play a radio or the TV. During the nighttime hours, keep several indoor lights on timers that have been set to various schedules.

As a finishing security touch, place a sign stating "Beware of Dog" in a prominent place. Whether you have a rottweiler or not, these signs often deter thieves.

## KEEPING RECORDS

Taking the simple precautions described so far will greatly reduce the chance that your home will be burglarized. But should it happen, filing a police report will be easier if you've kept a record of your valuables.

A record involves more than just making a list: You'll want to write down such particulars as the price, year, and place of purchase in addition to a detailed description of each item. This will help the police in the event of a burglary, and it will make it easier for you to file a claim on your household insurance policy. Be sure that you include serial numbers if the items have any. In the event that your stolen valuables are recovered, the serial numbers will give police positive identification so they can trace the items back to you.

Photograph or videotape the items for backup, then store this record where thieves are unlikely to look, such as in the garage or in the back of a child's closet. Better still: Store this information off-site, such as in a safe-deposit box.

Use an engraving pen to write your name, phone number, or other identifying information on your valuable appliances: TV, VCR, stereo, CD player, and your computer—including the housing of the internal hard disk drive. Engraving these items will make it harder for a thief to sell your stuff, and it links the objects to you should they ever be recovered.

# THE SIMPLE TRUTH
# ABOUT ALARMS

---*---

I F YOU HAVE A LARGE, VULNERABLE HOME OR PRICELESS POSSESSIONS INSIDE IT, YOU MAY OPT FOR A MORE PROACTIVE METHOD OF PROTECTION. THERE'S A SIMPLE SOLUTION: INSTALL AN ALARM SYSTEM.

There are do-it-yourself options, such as an exterior perimeter alarm that will shriek when your home is broken into. However, this type of system has you relying on your neighbors to take action should a break-in occur while you're away. The sound might scare off some burglars, but thieves today are hip to the fact that many law-abiding folks, jaded into complacency by the daily wail of false car and home alarms, tend to turn a deaf ear more often than they race to the telephone to call the authorities.

And should an intruder enter your home while you're inside it, such exterior systems (along with indoor sirens and infrared motion sensors) will certainly alert you to an intrusion the second it happens, but they won't summon outside help for you. A professional system, on the other hand, calls your home phone number moments after your alarm is triggered; if you don't respond, most companies will immediately dispatch a call to the local police. Besides, installing a do-it-yourself alarm system can

This old-fashioned alarm system is still one of the best—burglars think twice before breaking in where a dog resides.

## Arm Accessible Entry Points

You can save a bundle—and do it safely—when having a professional security system installed if you choose to have armed only those doors and windows that are easily accessible. If a window can't be reached without a ladder or other tools, simply lock it for safety and don't arm it. A burglar has no way of knowing which of your entry points will trigger the alarm.

require technical know-how, though virtually all come with detailed manuals and technical assistance by phone. If you're handy, you might want to give installation a go. You can find alarm systems through mail-order companies and at home-supply stores. Just buying a new dead-bolt lock or adding a few nails to your sliding glass door may be the cheapest safety measure, but a security system is far more effective. And while self-installed systems may be less expensive than professionally installed and monitored systems, they're also much less effective. A fully monitored system is the best value for your safety dollar.

## BRINGING IN THE PROS

Today's improved technology and competitive marketplace have made such systems more affordable than ever. And what do you get if you do decide to bring in the

security pros? Most systems include magnetic door and window contacts that trip the alarm when separated, a control keypad, and a siren alarm. In these systems, the central feature is an around-the-clock monitoring station that responds to any security breach by telephoning you. If you don't answer the call and provide your password, the police will be sent to your home. Should an intruder break in while you're there and force you to turn off the alarm, you can key in a special code that will send a silent call for help.

An alarm-system professional can also install handy features such as fire alarms and motion detectors, and panic buttons near your door or bed that silently summon police or medical help.

Most alarm systems are simple enough that a visitor or school-age child can learn how to operate them. Some systems allow you to assign temporary secondary codes so that a house guest can use your security system without knowing your master code.

**The central component of a monitored system is an around-the-clock station that will respond to any security breach by first telephoning you.**

Ultimately, the decision to install an alarm system in your home will hinge on how much security you need and whether you think the peace of mind that you stand to gain is worth the cost of a professionally installed and monitored alarm system.

If you're ready to take the plunge with a security professional, check under "Alarm

Systems" in the Yellow Pages or contact a crime-prevention specialist at your neighborhood police department and ask for a list of qualified companies in your area. Friends, neighbors, and insurance agents may also be able to give you names of a few reliable security companies.

You'll want to get at least three estimates, since prices and systems—as well as security advice—can vary dramatically from company to company.

Before scheduling an appointment to have your security needs assessed, make sure the company and its employees are trustworthy. Ask each company how its employees are trained and certified, and whether the company has the appropriate state or local licenses. As an added safety measure, consider scheduling the appointment for a time when another adult will be home. Ask for the name of the person who will be calling on you, and ask to see that person's company ID before admitting him or her into your home.

Once inside, the representative will inspect your home and ask questions about your schedule, your kids, and your pets. Your answers will guide the person in creating a system customized to your needs. During the visit, be sure to point out any valuable or irreplaceable items that bear special consideration: Great-Grandma's jewelry, the wine collection in the cellar, a child's baseball-card collection.

After completing its survey, the company should provide you with a written description of the system it recommends that you install, and a price quote for installation and monthly monitoring fees. Installation costs are usually based on the number of door and window contacts you have requested for your home.

---

## SIMPLE SOLUTIONS

# HOME SECURITY SYSTEMS

No SYSTEM FOR PROTECTING YOUR HOME is 100 percent effective, but these alternatives will markedly reduce the chance of a successful break-in. Remember that even the most sophisticated alarm system is of no use if you forget to set it.

**Simple**
Choose one from among the various kinds of do-it-yourself alarm systems on the market. Install the wires and contacts, test the system, then show everyone in your household how to use it.

**Simpler**
Use a combination of electric-light timers, dead-bolt door locks, outdoor lighting, and window locks to foil thieves. Be conscientious about locking your doors and windows.

**Simplest**
Have an alarm company install a system tailored to your home's layout and your family's schedule. Remember to arm the system at night and each time you leave the house.

# HEADING OFF DISASTER

---＊---

WHILE THEY MAY NEVER HAPPEN TO YOU, FIRES, FLOODS, EARTHQUAKES, TORNADOES, HURRICANES, AND OTHER CATASTROPHES STRIKE MILLIONS OF HOUSEHOLDERS EACH YEAR, SO IT'S ONLY PRUDENT TO PREPARE FOR THEM.

Assembling a disaster kit should be a top priority. Your kit should contain enough supplies to see your family through at least three days without basic services. While you can buy emergency kits, it's simpler and less expensive to create your own.

Start with a few basics: drinking water (about ½ gallon [approximately 2L] per person daily), canned or dried food, can opener, gas stove, current family photos (to help find family members who are missing), flashlights and radio with spare batteries, lantern, heavy-duty work gloves, candles, matches, and first-aid kit.

In addition, you should include flares or an alarm to summon emergency crews, a personal commode with sanitary bags, a

tarp, and several sturdy plastic lawn-and-leaf bags. A crowbar and shovel are useful if you need to work your way to a family member trapped by fallen objects. A hammer and nails will help secure your home's doors and windows if you must evacuate.

In addition, you should stash enough cash to see you through several days, as banks and automated teller machines may be shut down. If you have an infant, stock up on formula, diapers, and baby wipes. And if a family member requires medication, make sure you have an up-to-date supply on hand. Don't forget food, water, and a leash or cage for pets.

Store these supplies in a duffel bag or backpack that you can easily carry should

Prepare your home and family for anything
Mother Nature sends your way.

you have to evacuate. Keep all items that don't fit in the bag, such as water containers, in a place where they're easy to reach in a hurry. To the top of your kit, tape a "Don't Forget" list of last-minute items to take; such items might include an extra pair of glasses, your address book, important documents, and keepsakes.

## FIRE PRECAUTIONS

What do you need to make a home fire-safe? Mainly common sense: shutting off appliances after you've used them, keeping flammable items away from furnaces and space heaters, and making smoke detectors and fire extinguishers a part of your decor. The best extinguisher is an easy-to-handle 2- or 5-pound (1 or 2.5kg) model designed to put out most household fires. Place one in your kitchen and one in any other room where a fire might start.

Another simple safety precaution your family can take is to sleep with bedroom doors closed. Closed doors can keep smoke from spreading into these rooms, allowing you more time to escape.

Install a fireplace screen, and have your fireplace chimney and flue cleaned at least once a year. Maintain the kitchen stove in good working condition, and keep baking soda on hand to extinguish stove-top fires. In the garage, disconnect electrical tools and appliances when you're finished using them. Secure important papers in water- and fireproof strongboxes. Better yet: Put them in a safe-deposit box off-site.

Consider purchasing escape ladders for top-story bedrooms. And most important, practice fire drills with your family.

GETTING THEM ALL TOGETHER BEFORE DISASTER STRIKES WILL MAKE SURVIVAL EASIER FOR YOU AND YOUR FAMILY.

### Emergency kit

Use a watertight container to store a first-aid kit, canned food (and opener), a gas stove, cooking equipment, candles and matches, a portable radio, flashlights, and batteries.

### Light, water, shelter

Your emergency kit should also include a gas or battery-powered lantern and a waterproof tarp to shelter your family if you must evacuate your home. Plenty of drinking water (in unbreakable containers) is an absolute must; be sure to change it every few months.

## FLOODS

If you live in an area prone to floods, make sure to include life preservers with your disaster kit. If meteorologists issue a flood watch, meaning a flood may occur, move your furniture and valuables (time permitting) to a higher floor of your home. Then fill up your car at the gas station in case evacuation is necessary. If a flood warning is sounded, a flood is imminent. Turn on the radio or TV for weather updates and evacuation routes. Grab your emergency disaster kit, collect your valuables in large plastic bags, and get out.

## EARTHQUAKES

If your home lies in earthquake country, bolt bookcases, china cabinets, and other tall furniture to wall studs to prevent them from toppling onto family members in the event of a temblor. Store heavy objects on lower shelves where they are less likely to fall onto people. Fasten down lamps and other valuables with puttylike anchoring wax, and put latches on cabinet doors to keep the contents inside.

Just a few small things will make a big safety difference: Position your bed away from windows, which could shatter, and close the drapes or blinds at night to keep broken glass from flying into a bedroom. Resist the temptation to hang pictures over your bed or to store books, boxes, or other heavy items on a shelf above the bed.

In case an earthquake strikes at night, stash under your bed a pair of shoes in a plastic bag (broken glass may shower the floor). Next to them keep a flashlight and a crowbar to pry open jammed doors.

Make sure that all family members know how and when to shut off the water and gas valves. The main water valve (usually found near an exterior wall close to the water meter or the well supply) should be shut off immediately after a quake to prevent contamination of your home's water supply. Your gas valve (it's usually near the gas meter) should be off only if you smell gas or suspect a leak. Keep a wrench wired to the gas meter for this purpose.

## WIND AND RAIN

Whipping winds and rain—the effects of a hurricane or tornado can be devastating. Strong winds that enter a house through broken windows or a patio or garage door will weaken the structure of your home, exposing it to greater damage. To protect

**In an earthquake,** *loose objects may fall and shatter. If you secure breakables with anchoring wax, you can leave them on display.*

your windows from breaking, have storm shutters installed or create your own by buying precut sheets of 3/4-inch (2cm) plywood to fit each window. Make sure they fit snugly and can be attached onto the window quickly.

Many companies offer braces that will protect your vulnerable patio and garage doors from high winds. You might want to consider installing a new garage door that has been hurricane rated.

Many people don't think about the wind turbines that dot their roofs, though they're vulnerable to being blown off during high winds and will leave a gaping hole for rain to come in. Make sure there are no leaks in your roof, and check the wind turbine regularly. Consider replacing the turbine with a style of wind vent that is less vulnerable to violent gusts.

Keep large plastic trash bags and drop cloths on hand to spread over furniture, computers, and other home valuables in the event that your roof springs a leak.

**Wind that enters through broken windows or a patio or garage door will weaken your home's structure, exposing it to much greater damage.**

During storm season, clear your yard of all loose objects—such as potted plants, bicycles, trash cans, and patio furniture—that can become flying lethal weapons in the grip of a raging storm.

Finally, make sure you and your family have a personal evacuation plan in the event of a hurricane, and a safe zone in

## Shutting Off the Gas

If you smell gas after a disaster strikes, turn off the gas at the main shutoff valve next to your gas meter. Use a wrench to give the valve a quarter turn clockwise or counterclockwise; when the tang (the part you put the wrench on) is perpendicular to the pipe, the valve is closed.

your home in case of a tornado. Determine where or how you'll find each other should a hurricane hit. Choose several places—a friend's home in another town, a shelter, or a motel. Each family member should keep handy the phone numbers of your designated spots and a local road map: If your regular routes are clogged or closed, you may need to take unfamiliar roads.

Before a tornado is headed your way, pick a spot in your building where family members can gather in relative safety. It might be your basement; if there is no basement, choose a hallway, bathroom, or closet on the lowest floor. Keep this place free of clutter. If you're in an apartment building, you may not have enough time to go to the bottom floor. Instead, pick a location in a hallway or under a staircase in the center of your building.

You're at the mercy of Mother Nature when she unleashes her strongest elements, but with just a bit of preparation, you can easily keep your family—and your home —safe in the event of a natural disaster.

# LESS-STRESS
# Redecorating

—✳—

**1** Combine **inviting colors** and interesting fabrics and textures. Mix the traditional with the unexpectedly novel. **2** Before you shop for new furnishings, **rearrange** what you have. Artful regrouping will often provide an exciting new look. **3** Group like items **together** where they will have the most impact on a room. **4** Decorative objects with a **reflective** quality—glass, mirrors, metal—add distinctive highlights to a room. **5** For a romantic look in your **bedroom,** drape fabric over curtain rods, furniture, or the headboard. **6** For more spacious-looking **bathrooms,** remove mats from floors and furry covers from commodes. **7** When you shop for **furnishings,** make sure that they do not require more upkeep than you have the time to provide. **8** Select **window coverings** that complement the room and are easy to keep clean. **9** Before calling a **professional designer,** consider your needs, preferences, schedule, and budget. **10** When giving a **party,** choose decorations that carry out a unified theme. ●

# EASY HOME DECORATING

## FAST FACE-LIFTS AND ARTFUL ADDITIONS

\* —— \* —— \*

Nesting—that most pleasurable business of making a house a home—is rarely as easy as professional decorators make it look. Nevertheless, you can put the pros' winning design strategies to work in your home—without enrolling in design school or signing on the dotted line.

Simply by rearranging your household possessions with the eye of a designer—repositioning furniture, artwork, and accessories in a manner that brings everything into focus—you can easily give your home a fresh new look.

Add a few accents that pack a big design punch—a flea market find, a beautiful new throw blanket, pillows in that hot new color—and you're well on your way to creating a home that is more beautiful and enjoyable.

Take advantage of a few simple tricks that professional designers use, and you can simplify the art of making your home a reflection of your own personal taste and style.

# EVERYTHING OLD
# IS NEW AGAIN

——————— ✳ ———————

I S YOUR LIVING ROOM LESS THAN LIVELY? YOUR BATHROOM BLAND? YOUR BEDROOM BORING? CHANCES ARE YOUR SEEMINGLY STALE ROOMS ALREADY CONTAIN ALL THE RIGHT ELEMENTS TO MAKE THEM WARM AND VIBRANT.

It may be that all they need is some artful and imaginative rearranging of furniture and accessories to pull it all together.

As you evaluate your rooms, consider everything in your home as raw material for a new and improved decor. Bring that lovely Chinese water pitcher out of hiding in the china cabinet and place it center stage atop the fireplace mantel. Replace it with an equally unexpected treasure each year to keep the living room looking fresh.

## THE LIVING ROOM

Even the most beautiful furnishings won't work together if they're not arranged in a way that beckons you to come in and sit a spell. And decorative objects that are poorly placed or lost amid neighboring items often look extraneous rather than ornamental. When it comes to interior design, the number one rule is that the arrangement of a room's contents is nearly as important as the contents themselves.

**The idea is not to adhere slavishly to a particular style,
but to project your own taste and personality.**

Mix things up for warm touches that unite the past and present, such as an antique side table paired up with a comfy new sofa. The idea is not to adhere slavishly to a particular style or era—such as Victorian or Mission—but to project your own taste and personality. After all, who really wants a room that looks as if everything arrived on the same delivery truck?

The designer-inspired strategies on the next few pages can help you evaluate each room in your home and reorganize the items within it. The goal is to maximize design impact while creating spaces that are both comfortable and livable.

How do you know if your furniture placement needs some professional polish? Take a look around your living room—is your furniture flush against the walls? To create a sense of depth and softness, you should position furniture at an angle or floating away from the wall. This makes the room feel less boxy, more intimate and inviting.

Start by placing the largest piece, usually the sofa, so it faces the room's main focal point, such as a window with a view or a fireplace. Next, group the rest of the seating a maximum of 10 feet (3m) from the sofa—farther away makes conversation while seated difficult. Balance pieces of a similar size by placing them across from each other. For example, a pair of upholstered chairs placed opposite the sofa will provide a better balance than would a pair of delicate wooden chairs. Within your conversational circle, allow 3 feet (1m) between pieces for easy traffic flow into and out of the seating area.

Balance the room by putting major elements on separate walls; the television armoire will be more prominent if it isn't right next to the fireplace. Place darker pieces where they'll get the most light, by a window or floor lamp—a dark cabinet will disappear in a dimly lit corner.

If the room is large, set up a secondary area to make the room feel cozier and do double duty: Add a desk and chair to a window corner, or create a family game area with a small table and a few chairs.

To create the illusion of more space in a smaller room, place the furniture, starting with the sofa, on a corner diagonal. This unusual placement takes the focus off the room size and places it on the furnishings instead. Resist the urge to fill up the room with every stick of furniture you own. Bare areas imply spaciousness.

Whatever your living room's size, you should arrange its furniture in a way that makes living comfortable. If you plan to use it for entertaining, are there enough places where guests can set down glasses and plates? If a coffee table is out of reach from some chairs, place small tables beside them. Will you be watching Humphrey Bogart classics from your sofa? If so, make sure there's a shelf or cabinet nearby with space to store your videotapes of *Casablanca* and *The Maltese Falcon*.

Rearranging your furnishings is a simple yet effective way to give a room a new look.

## DECORATIVE OBJECTS

Now that you've got the foundation—your furniture—in place, it's time to consider the placement of your decorative objects. Your collections, artwork, and photographs are the elements that project your personality into a room. Why not show them off as a designer would, making the most of each piece of furniture?

Start with the walls. Is your picture arrangement boring? Consider rehanging your wall treasures in asymmetrical groupings rather than in straightforward rows; this creates a sense of drama. Place the bottom edge of the lowest piece 6 to 8 inches (15–20cm) above the top of the furniture; work upward from there, going as high as you like. Hang petite groupings behind a dainty table or chair, a large single picture in back of your ample sofa.

A multitude of tiny treasures spread about a room may seem homey, but the overall effect is usually unfocused rather than appealing. Instead, group items that

have a similar texture, shape, or theme together on shelves, on a coffee table or end table, atop the armoire—and leave a hand's breadth or more of space between each grouping for maximum effect.

Consider your plant placement. If you've stashed that lovely ficus or palm tree in the corner, bring it out! Ideally, plants should enhance something nearby, such as a chair or a lamp, instead of looking like an afterthought.

If your room is dark, here's a simple way to lighten it up: Purchase a trio of inexpensive ready-made mirrors, and add ornate or interesting frames. The frames should have a common element, such as a similar shape, finish, or theme: If you're going Victorian, choose a trio of similarly ornate, perhaps gilded, frames; if you're after an Art Deco feel, three floral motifs will work nicely together. Mirrors bring light and depth to a room. For the greatest benefit, hang your mirrors with their horizontal center just a bit higher than eye level on the wall opposite or adjacent to a window. As an alternative, install several small wall-mounted spotlights positioned to shine down on your favorite pictures or your splendid shell collection.

Finally, take a tip from home-design magazines and designers themselves: Any room quickly becomes both brighter and more inviting when you add a cozy throw blanket, a sparkling crystal vase or sculpture, or a polished brass or gilded picture frame. By adding a few of these, and by making the most of what you already have inside the room, you can give your home professional design polish.

## Vintage Beauty

Don't toss something away just because it is weathered or aged—meaningful pieces that show the inevitable signs of long life add richness to any room. The loveliest rooms are those that combine something old, treasured, and well worn alongside a few new things.

# EASY WEEKEND FACE-LIFTS

✳

**W**HAT A DIFFERENCE A DAY (OR TWO) MAKES! Like a perfect candidate for a makeover, a tired-looking room may benefit from a nip and tuck here, a little added color and pizzazz there. A weekend spent updating your home—no major surgery required— makes it a fresher, brighter place to come home to on Monday.

**Eye-catching slipcovers** *give the chairs in your din- ing room a fresh new look. Just slip the covers over the chairs for updated elegance in minutes.*

**A large potted plant** *instantly makes any space more inviting. Choose a plant that will adapt to the level of sunlight in its new environment.*

**Add to your storage space** *with panache by placing attractive baskets beneath a glass coffee table. Fill them with magazines or folded throw blankets.*

**Put natural style** *in your bathroom by filling a pretty glass bowl with seashells and placing it next to the sink.*

## Lightening Up

Color is the most obvious—and most indispensable—decorating element. And paint is an inexpensive and easily changeable way to dramatize walls. To add depth and minimize the illusion of space in a room, use deep, rich colors like terra-cotta, forest green, and blue. To make a room seem larger, use lighter colors such as yellow, pink, and cream.

### BRIGHTER BATHROOMS

When it comes to making the most of your bathroom, less is definitely more. Control countertop chaos by corralling personal hygiene items into interesting containers, baskets, or boxes. Nothing makes a space seem smaller than it is than having items spilling from every surface.

Remove that little throw rug on the bathroom floor to give an illusion of more space. And strip the commode of its furry cover to keep it from becoming the room's focal point. Why dress up the one fixture to which you least want to call attention? To make the room appear less utilitarian, bring in a wooden chest or a few stacking wicker or rattan boxes to add character as well as storage space. If you have a folding screen languishing in a closet somewhere, place it between the sink and toilet to add a bit of style along with privacy.

If your bathroom is without windows, add mirrors to the walls and choose bright, cheery colors for the bath and hand towels to give the room an airier, more spacious feel. Paint or stain the cabinets in a color that complements your towels. Or install new handles and knobs—a bright color, silver, or white matte. It's a great way to add flair without taking up any space.

Finally, if you have exposed pipes in the bathroom, paint them the same color as the walls, or paint on a faux finish in complementary colors. Since you can't get rid of the pipes, make the most of them.

### COZIER KITCHENS

Amid the congestion of the fridge and the stove, table and chairs, and hardworking countertops, kitchens usually have little leftover space for decorative touches. Still, you can add character to this functional room by using the treasures you probably already have in your home.

For a homey touch, arrange cooking utensils in a decorative ceramic vase rather than a plastic holder. Stash the sponge and scrubber in a small painted pot instead of leaving them strewn haphazardly on the countertop. Hang bright dish towels from the refrigerator or oven handle to add a splash of color to the room.

Such little pick-me-ups can pack a big design punch. Freshen up the kitchen by placing baskets, bowls, or other decorative containers on a windowsill or countertop near the sink, or atop your breakfast table or fridge. Fill them with seasonal accents: gourds in autumn, chestnuts in winter, bright lemons in spring, limes in summer. Of course, fresh flowers can perk up the room any time of year. Even a bird feeder outside the window lends life and color.

Is your kitchen on the plain side? For a quick fix, replace your humdrum cabinet and drawer handles with chrome or brass hardware or colorful plastic fittings. Paint or stain the cabinets, or the entire room, in a bold new color. It's the quickest and cheapest way to transform your kitchen—and should you decide you don't like it, you can easily change the color later.

And speaking of quick changes, does your kitchen table seem to take over the room? You should optimally have at least 3 feet (1m) of passageway between the table and the adjoining walls or appliances. If your table is too large, replace it with a smaller one. What you'll lose in serving area you will gain in mealtime intimacy.

## BETTER BEDROOMS

This is one room that you'd like to have feel as luxurious and comfortable as possible when you and your significant other settle in each evening. Start by editing out what you can—say, an extra chair or a dresser—and rearranging the furnishings that you keep. Change the color of the bed linens and add a couple of brightly colored pillows to the bed or chairs.

For a romantic look, drape swags or other fabric treatments over curtain rods, furniture, or the headboard. If you have a four-poster bed, try creating a canopy by hanging inexpensive mosquito netting from the ceiling. Look for an unusual pair of lamps the next time you're browsing in

an antique store or flea market—changing the bedside lamps is an easy fix that will quickly alter the feel of a room.

Add whimsy to children's bedrooms with a bit of fabric, a can or two each of fabric paint and wall paint, and some creativity. You can personalize the bed ruffle or the curtains by stenciling them with flowers, princesses, trucks, cars, or bears.

**For a romantic look in your bedroom, drape fabric over curtain rods, furniture, or the headboard.**

Paint kids' bookshelves a favorite color, then put baskets painted in a contrasting shade on the shelves for extra storage. To dress up the windows, add a ready-made lace or eyelet panel above the blinds, then tie it to one side. Or try using two plain panels in a bold color that hang from a rod so kids can pull them aside easily.

**A richly patterned shawl** *adds drama when draped over a bed. Such colorful accents can easily be changed to refresh the look of your room and add a luxurious touch.*

# THE SIMPLE ART
# OF FURNISHING

---- * ----

WHETHER YOU DELIGHT IN THE OPULENCE OF VICTORIAN FURNISHINGS OR PREFER THE SPARSENESS OF A MODERN LOOK, OUTFITTING YOUR HOME WITH NEW FURNITURE AND FLOOR COVERINGS CAN BE SIMPLE.

Your additions should fit your taste and lifestyle, be easy to maintain, and, most important, fit within your budget. It pays to shop carefully, since your selections will be a part of your home for years to come. Here are some guidelines for simplifying your selection of furniture, window treatments, and floor coverings.

If you have children, consider getting well-made wooden or wicker furniture that can be easily wiped clean of crumbs, spills, and fingerprints; and upholstered couches with sturdy frames that can withstand

If kids aren't a design consideration, go ahead and indulge yourself with those pretty yet vulnerable furnishings on your wish list. But keep in mind that ornately carved wooden pieces and dreamy silk or satin upholstery can be a nightmare to keep clean and fresh looking.

One useful rule for homes, with or without kids: Buy the best furnishings you can afford. A sturdy, well-made sofa or top-of-the-line, stain-resistant carpet usually will last longer and look better than an alternative of lesser quality. Also,

**Opt for patterned area rugs in lieu of solid-colored carpeting; the patterns hide the inevitable spills and spots of daily family life.**

repeated trouncing from your kids. Pick durable fabrics—such as cotton and linen chenille, tightly woven cotton, or upholstered nylon—that are relatively easy to maintain or can be treated with a stain-resistant chemical. In lieu of solid-colored wall-to-wall carpeting, opt for patterned area rugs that have a slip-proof backing; the patterns will hide the inevitable spills and spots of daily family life. If you have wall-to-wall carpeting, a professional cleaning every three to six months will help keep it looking its best.

be sure to ask how best to maintain the floor covering or furniture you're considering; correct care can prolong its life.

## SMARTER SHOPPING

It's never been easier to find the perfect sofa or chair for your home. There are so many styles from which to choose: the traditional look of the Colonial style, with its pine, oak, cherry, and maple pieces; the clean, straight lines of Mission-style furniture; the sleek, geometric lines of 1920's and 1930's Art Deco; the spartan shapes and designs of Modern furnishings; the whimsy of Postmodernism; and the anything-goes appeal of the eclectic look.

Which sofa is best for your home? A sofa's back is the one element that has the greatest effect on how the couch looks and feels; that is where you should start inspecting the lovely piece that has particularly caught your eye.

There are four main styles to consider: the firm, upright variety; the sofa with an attached pillow back; the kind that has removable pillows; and the style that features multiple pillows you can rearrange to your taste for customized comfort.

Once you've selected the back style that best suits your tastes, take a careful look at the sofa frame. Today you'll find good long-lasting frames in steel, plastic, laminate, or a combination of materials —and many of these frames are tough enough that even the most rambunctious of children can't damage them. Choose the frame that passes the comfort test and has the lines you find most pleasing. The rest of your decision will be purely esthetic and personal: the style of the sofa's base (such as skirted or upholstered), the base and arm styles, and the fabric. Whatever fabric you choose, having the upholsterer protect it with a stain repellent should considerably extend the life and beauty of the piece in your home.

Chairs, whether upholstered or not, should be similarly comfortable. A chair's firmness, depth, and back height all have a bearing on how you'll feel while sitting or lounging there. Sit a spell before you buy, putting your feet up or placing throw pillows just as you would if you were at home. If the chair doesn't feel right in the store, it never will in your living room.

**Swathed in white fabric,** *a pine bedstead lends country charm to a bedroom that is simple yet comfortable. Flowers in a rustic terra-cotta vase add warmth.*

# PICK-ME-UP FURNISHINGS

DOES YOUR HOME GIVE YOU THE BLAHS? A few simple additions can help brighten up your rooms—and your mood—in no time. These artful, easy-to-add items can transform a lifeless living room, a boring bath, a dull hallway, or a lackluster kitchen into a place where your style and personality shine through.

**Update a worn couch** *in minutes by draping it with a casual yet stylish slipcover. Some covers tie in place at the corners to fit a variety of couch styles.*

**A bathroom caddy** *displays towels where guests can easily find them, and also adds counter space.*

**A rollout kitchen island** *provides both a surface for chopping and preparing and extra shelves for holding pots, vegetables, cookbooks, and condiments.*

**Skirt an old table**—*or a cardboard table—with fabric for an instant touch of elegance. Store items under the skirt.*

## WONDERFUL WINDOWS

Window coverings are a quick way to alter the look and feel of any room. There are so many styles from which to choose—horizontal and vertical blinds, draperies, shades, sheers, shutters, wood blinds.

**If possible, buy draperies from a company that offers in-home measuring—this will keep you from making costly mistakes.**

Each offers a distinctive look—and price range. Miniblinds are generally the least expensive; custom fabric shades—such as Roman and balloon—the most costly. You'll need to consider two things before you go shopping: how much you'd like to spend, and which look and fabric is right for the room. For example, plastic blinds are an excellent choice for the kitchen and the bathroom, as they're easy to wipe free of dirt and grime and won't be damaged by heat or humidity.

In general, simple is best. Windows covered with ruffles to the rafters quickly get tired-looking—not to mention dusty. Most shops for window coverings offer a wide variety of styles, with equally varied prices. If you're just looking for a simple miniblind treatment for the bath, most dealers can provide dozens of options (macro, mini, horizontal, and vertical) in many colors and materials, such as plastic, wood, or metal. But measure carefully if you're installing the blinds yourself; unless your window is a standard size, you will need to special order the blinds.

If you're looking for fabric draperies, plan to shop around and compare prices and design advice before you sign on the dotted line. If possible, select a company that offers guaranteed in-home measuring—this will keep you from making any costly mistakes. Most shops will provide an in-house decorating consultant to help you find the perfect fabric and style, but the advice—and the prices for the window coverings—will vary from store to store.

## FABULOUS FLOORS

The many flooring options available today include vinyl, ceramic tile, laminate, and wood—what's the right choice for you?

When shopping for flooring, consider durability first. If you have a family, you'll

**Versatile and practical,** *blinds are a favorite for every room in the house. Few other window coverings provide such precise control over both light and privacy.*

**Wood floors,** *common in older homes, are warm, durable, and easy to keep clean. Area rugs can provide focus in seating spaces.*

You'll also be wise to consider moisture resistance if you'll be covering your bathroom or kitchen floors. The more grooves and seams the floor has, the easier it is for water to find its way beneath the floor

**You'll want to know if the flooring material you're considering will stand up to repeated trampling, spills, and cleaning.**

covering and cause expensive damage. If you're going the ceramic-tile route, don't skimp on the installation by having your Uncle Fred lay it for you. It's imperative that tile be evenly laid and properly sealed to prevent water damage.

Glazed ceramic tiles are a good choice for kitchen and bathroom floors: They are water-resistant, and in the event of damage you can replace the individual tiles without having to redo the entire floor.

want to know if the material you're considering will stand up to repeated trampling, spills, and cleaning. One good choice for the kitchen, bathroom, living room, and dining room is vinyl flooring, which is available in an enormous range of colors and patterns, some designed to look like granite, marble, wood, and other natural materials. All vinyl floors are coated with several layers of clear vinyl or urethane that serve as a protective shield against wear and are resistant to moisture.

Next you need to consider your budget. If you want to save by installing the floor yourself, consider vinyl floors, which come in tiles or rolls. Some vinyl tiles come with peel-off backing for easy installation; this makes them the simplest choice for the do-it-yourselfer on a shoestring.

## Ideas from Design Magazines

Looking to give your bedroom decor a lift or to spice up the kitchen walls? Visit a bookstore and pick up a few home-design magazines. They're chock-full of beautiful interiors—and they're a cost-effective source of up-to-the-minute design ideas.

# IF YOU DESIRE A DESIGNER

---✳---

THE RIGHT HOME DESIGNER IS LIKE A SERENELY PATIENT MOM OR DAD WHO LISTENS TO YOUR WANTS, NEEDS, AND DREAMS—AND THEN HELPS YOU BRING THEM TO LIFE IN A COST-, TIME-, AND COMFORT-EFFICIENT MANNER.

If you're ready to take the plunge and hire a professional to decorate your home, the process will be smoother and more enjoyable if you're prepared to explain what you like and want. After all, who wants to pay a decorator for three hours of shopping time that result in a choice of colors, fabrics, and furnishings that don't appeal to you? Before you pick up the telephone, here are several simple things that you can do to streamline the process.

*Start a home file.* Create a list of your personal likes and dislikes in home decor. Do you enjoy the relaxed feeling of contemporary furnishings and found objects, or do you prefer the polished, ornate elegance of rich Victorian colors and fabrics? Jot down what works for you—and what

doesn't. A clear list that your designer can refer to while shopping for you will help him or her bring back furniture pictures, color palettes, and fabric swatches that will be an appropriate match for you and your home—the first time around.

*Consider your needs for each room.* Does your living room have to double as a family room? Do the kids need a place to do homework in the kitchen? Let your designer know all the activities that will go on inside the rooms you are decorating. A good designer can help you create the space for it all, beautifully.

**This multipurpose great room** *feels spacious and intimate at the same time, thanks to design elements that define separate areas for eating, cooking, and socializing.*

*Collect pictures.* Flip through a few home design magazines and tear out the pages with photographs that catch your eye. You don't have to want everything inside the room—including the colors and fabrics—but if the overall feeling of the room works for you, have it ready to show the interior designer. Conversely, if you happen upon a room that just leaves you cold, tear out that page to show to the designer, too. This information will tell him or her what you *don't* want to see, which will save time and effort for both of you.

*Create a timetable.* If you want to do your whole house—or even one room—in phases, be sure to let the designer know that at the start. You don't have to do it all,

or spend your entire design budget, in a few short weeks. Spread the design process out over months or even years so you and your designer can take advantage of liquidations and seasonal sales—and help you

**Know how much money you can spend, and make sure your designer knows, too. A good designer will work within your guidelines.**

get more for less. Conversely, if you need to have that remodeled kitchen or bathroom beautiful and operational in time for the holidays or an important dinner party, let your designer know that as well.

*Establish a budget.* Know how much money you can comfortably spend, and make sure your designer knows, too. A good designer will work within your guidelines—and let you know if your plans or your budget need adjusting.

Now that you're ready to find the perfect designer, where do you look? If you admire the home decor of a neighbor or friend, ask if a designer was involved. (If one wasn't, your question will be taken as a compliment!) Or call an interior design association for references (for a starting place, see pages 142–143).

You should interview at least three designers, take a close look at each one's portfolio, and call former clients before you sign on the dotted line. During each interview, gauge just how well you and the designer communicate. Choose the person with whom you are most comfortable and whose style best suits your ideas.

# SIMPLY PUT...

### DESIGNERSPEAK

**ASID** • Acronym for the American Society of Interior Designers. It's appended to the names of designers who have met rigorous qualification standards that include design education, work experience, and a two-day examination by the National Council for Interior Design Qualification.

**color board** • A designer's presentation of several color groupings of fabric, carpeting, paint, and flooring for you to choose from when decorating.

**portfolio** • A collection of photographs, and possibly sketches and floor plans, showing examples of a designer's prior work for other clients.

# MAKING YOUR HOME PARTY-FRIENDLY

———— ✳ ————

W HAT MAKES A HOME PARTY-FRIENDLY? DECORATIONS ARE AN IMPORTANT PART OF SETTING THE MOOD, BUT HOW YOUR HOME IS ARRANGED AND WHERE YOU PLACE THE FOOD AND DRINKS ALSO PLAY A CRUCIAL ROLE.

These ingredients can mean the difference between a fete that's a fabulous whirl of sparkling conversation and activity and a less-than-lively, staid affair.

Parties offer a chance to launch new friendships, and if you make it easy for people to talk to each other by creating space for the festivities ahead, everything else will simply fall into place.

## PARTY SPACES

Whether your home is spacious or small, if you're having a large party you'll want to make room for your guests in the party areas—the living room, dining room, and family room—of your home. If necessary, roll 'em up and move 'em out: Remove an area rug from your living room to clear out space for dancing; haul the big furnishings, like the sofa and ottoman, out of the living room and place them behind closed doors in another room. Or you can just push the furniture against the walls to open up more floor space and ease circulation.

After all, a lively gathering is one that encourages people to meet new friends, and with more space in which to wander, your guests will feel more relaxed. One key strategy for keeping everyone active: Have fewer chairs than people. With the

exception of dinner parties, a party stops being festive as soon as everyone is seated. Remove the dining room chairs, and let the table serve as an hors d'oeuvres station. Keep your guests circulating through your home: Place the refreshments in one room, the buffet in another, and the desserts and coffee in a third area or room.

For small groups, limit the party to just one or two rooms of your house and

*Festive decor is one key to a successful party. Holiday lights and decorations set a warm, welcoming tone for your guests.*

SIMPLE TOUCHES LIKE THESE CAN ADD A FESTIVE NOTE THAT GUESTS DETECT EVEN BEFORE YOU OPEN THE DOOR TO WELCOME THEM INSIDE.

### Door wreath

Whatever the season, make guests feel welcome with a door wreath that incorporates flowers, leaves, herbs, or fruits tied with a ribbon. You can buy ready-made wreaths or make your own by adding a few inexpensive seasonal touches to a base of artificial greenery or dried vines.

### Festoons

For a shower or holiday party, hang swags of plant materials or indoor-outdoor ribbon from the handrail of your porch or front steps.

### Tree lights

Entwine strings of tiny lights around outdoor shrubs or small trees to brighten your entryway on a dark winter night. Or twist lights around twigs in a large vase that you set in your front window as a welcoming beacon for guests.

### Votive candles

Beckon guests into your home by placing a trail of votive candles—in glass holders or weighted paper bags—on the walkway to your front door.

direct guests to the bathroom you want them to use. Avoid opening your den or upstairs rooms to guests. Once the group disperses into your home's outer reaches, cliques will form that may make some of your guests feel left out.

Your party should be a reflection of you, so choose a theme that makes you feel bright and alive. Exaggerate a single element—if pink's your theme color, scatter pink balloons about the house or fill vases with pink roses; greet arrivals with a rosy drink. For a Mexican fiesta, place a different piñata on the food table in every room; serve drinks in margarita glasses.

## THE BIG PICTURE

Remember to look at the whole picture—lighting, texture, scale, and progression (such as pots of flowers lining the front

**Tickle guests' senses with imaginative surprises: a soaring centerpiece, glitter scattered on a walkway, or floating gardenias.**

walk). Fill your home with background music that's appropriate for the party's theme: classical for sit-down dinner parties, salsa for spirited celebrations. Dim the lights for a more intimate mood. The senses should be tickled by imaginative surprises: a centerpiece that soars above the buffet table, glitter scattered along a walkway, gardenias floating in glass bowls. And remember—you'll enjoy yourself and your guests more if you finish decorating well in advance of party time.

# CHECKLISTS
## AND RESOURCES

### INFORMATION FOR HOUSEHOLDERS

\* —— \* —— \*

There's much to be said for making a list and checking it twice. Doing your homework before you get on the phone or head down the aisles of a home-improvement store can make every household project more efficient.

The handy checklists in this section will get you started on some of the more common household tasks you're likely to undertake. They provide everything from repair and maintenance logs to questions you should ask cleaning services and design professionals before you sign on the dotted line. Simply write their answers directly on these pages, or photocopy the lists to use again and again.

The resources at the end of this section provide names of publications, suppliers, and organizations that will help you successfully complete the project at hand. Knowing where to turn for additional facts or useful products will help you make the most of your time and effort.

# BUDGET SAVERS

## MAKING EVERY PENNY COUNT

———————— ✳ ————————

KEEPING YOUR HOUSEHOLD UP AND RUNNING CAN COST A BUNDLE. BUT IF YOU CONSULT THIS LIST BEFORE BUYING SUPPLIES OR TURNING ON POWER-HUNGRY APPLIANCES, YOU CAN SAVE A PILE OF CASH.

### SHOPPING

- Purchase only what you need.
- Buy products in bulk.
- Clip—and use—coupons.
- Choose dual-purpose cleaners.
- Select energy-efficient lightbulbs.
- Purchase laundry products with boosters, such as color-safe bleach.

### STORAGE AND ORGANIZATION

- Fill suitcases and trunks with out-of-season clothes.
- Use baskets and ceramic mugs as catchalls for odds and ends.

### ENERGY CONSUMPTION

- Turn off all unnecessary lights.
- Lower the thermostat to 68°F (20°C) in winter; raise it to 78°F (26°C) in summer.
- Lower your water heater's setting to 120°F (49°C).
- Use your microwave instead of the conventional oven for reheating.

- Choose the smallest pan for the job.
- Turn off electric burners shortly before the end of allotted cooking time.
- Preheat your oven only if the recipe you're using calls for it.
- Use a pressure cooker when you're making soups and stews.
- Cover water that you've set to boil.
- Run appliances at night or on weekends when rates are lower.
- Select the cold rinse for your laundry.
- Use your dishwasher's Light Wash cycle for lightly soiled dishes.
- Choose the dishwasher's Cool Dry setting instead of Hot Dry.

**Small economies can add up to big savings.**

# HOUSEHOLD ORGANIZATION

## GETTING IT ALL TOGETHER

I T SHOULD BE NO SURPRISE THAT THE SECRET TO GETTING ORGANIZED IS TO
TAKE AN ORDERLY APPROACH: PRUNE AWAY THE EXCESS, STOW WHAT'S LEFT
IN LOGICAL PLACES, AND RESOLVE TO KEEP CLUTTER FROM BUILDING UP AGAIN.

### 1. WHAT SHOULD I KEEP?

*Ask yourself:*

☐ Have I used or enjoyed this recently?

☐ Does someone in the family value this?

☐ Would I save it if there were a fire?

☐ Will I need this later?

*(If you checked one or more of the above
boxes, keep it!)*

### 2. WHERE DOES IT GO?

*Place articles in five bags or boxes labeled:*

◆ Other rooms

◆ Give away

◆ Toss or recycle

◆ Storage

◆ Garage sale

### 3. HOW SHOULD I ORGANIZE
### THE KEEPERS?

*Use these organizing principles for stashing
the stuff you're keeping:*

◆ Create a place for every item.

◆ Store things near where you'll use them.

◆ Place least-used items on top shelves.

◆ Keep like items together.

◆ Corral small objects in baskets.

◆ Stack stored items in similar-size
boxes to maximize space.

◆ Label each storage container.

### 4. HOW CAN I CONTROL
### CLUTTER IN THE FUTURE?

*Make these strategies a part of your life:*

◆ Place a catchall basket in your home's
busiest rooms to hold keys, receipts,
mail, and other items until you can
find the time to organize them.

◆ Place baskets at the bottom and top of
the stairs to hold things that belong on
another floor; take one or more items
with you when going up or down.

◆ When you bring home a new shirt, a
kitchen knickknack, or a toy for the kids,
resolve to store, recycle, give away, or toss
another item that's past its prime.

◆ Make putting away playthings a part
of your child's nightly bedtime ritual.

◆ Set aside 15 minutes each day to return
mislaid books, magazines, cups, and
so forth to their rightful homes.

◆ Spend an extra minute each night
to hang up your coat, fold your T-shirt
or sweater, put away your pants, and
stow your loafers in your closet.

◆ Keep your significant other current
on important engagements, school
information, bills due, and invitations
to respond to, by putting the papers in
a special folder or "hot-stuff" basket.

# HOME SAFETY AND SECURITY

## HEADING OFF HOUSEHOLD HAZARDS

＊

SOME THREATS TO YOUR FAMILY'S SAFETY YOU CAN DETECT BEFORE THEY CAUSE HARM; OTHERS DO THEIR DAMAGE WITHOUT WARNING. PREPARE FOR BOTH WITH THIS CHECKLIST (ALSO SEE CHILDPROOFING TIPS, PAGE 134).

### EMERGENCIES

☐ Buy or assemble a first-aid kit.

☐ Prepare a disaster survival kit.

☐ Keep emergency numbers by the phone.

### ACCIDENT PREVENTION

☐ Make sure entrances are well lit.

☐ Keep walkways, stairs, and halls clear.

☐ Place nonslip stickers or a mat on the bottom of the tub.

☐ Turn down the hot water heater to 120°F (49°C).

☐ Place flashlights in guest rooms.

### FIRE SAFETY

☐ Keep a fire extinguisher in the kitchen, workshop, garage, and near bedrooms.

☐ Install smoke detectors in all bedrooms, outside their doors, and in hallways leading to them; at tops of stairs; in basement den or office. Test monthly; replace batteries annually.

☐ Keep bedroom doors closed at night.

### ENVIRONMENTAL HAZARDS

☐ *Asbestos:* Give it a wide berth if it's intact; call an expert if it crumbles.

☐ *Carbon monoxide:* Install detectors and make sure batteries are fresh.

☐ *Lead paint:* Test old painted surfaces for lead; if they contain it, paint or wallpaper over them.

☐ *Radon gas:* Test for it and have it eliminated if necessary.

### SECURITY

☐ Trim back bushes and trees near windows and doors.

☐ Remove ladders, trash cans, and garden tools from the yard.

☐ Coat metal drainpipes up to the second floor with petroleum jelly to keep burglars from climbing the pipes.

☐ Install motion-sensor lights outside.

☐ Add locks to first- and second-story windows. (In bedrooms, leave one window lock-free to serve as an emergency exit.)

☐ Put a broom handle or metal bar in tracks of sliding-glass doors (unless door is an emergency exit).

☐ Replace hollow-core front doors with metal or solid wood.

☐ Install a high-quality dead-bolt lock on the front door.

☐ Add timers to indoor lights, TVs, and stereos and set them to go on and off at different times of the day.

# KITCHEN SAFETY

## HANDLING AND STORING FOOD SAFELY

——— ✳ ———

KEEP GERMS AND BACTERIA IN CHECK—AND OUT OF YOUR FOOD—BY TAKING THESE PRECAUTIONS IN THE KITCHEN. WHEN IT COMES TO THE HEALTH OF YOUR FAMILY AND GUESTS, YOU CAN NEVER BE TOO CAREFUL.

### DEFROSTING

- In the refrigerator: Thaw frozen meat overnight; large cuts may take longer.
- On the countertop: Place meat in a watertight plastic bag and submerge in a bowl of cold water. Leave just until thawed, changing the water every 30 minutes. Cook or refrigerate promptly.
- In the microwave: Use the defrost setting, then finish cooking immediately.

### FOOD HANDLING

- Wipe cooking surfaces clean with hot, soapy water before and after cooking; rinse the surfaces thoroughly; dry well with paper towels.
- Wash hands (with soap and hot, running water) before preparing food and after touching raw meat.
- Wear rubber gloves if there are cuts or sores on your hands.
- Use separate cutting boards for meats and nonmeats (or disinfect with mild bleach solution between uses).
- When pounding meat or chicken, cover with a layer of plastic wrap to avoid splattering juices.
- Wash (with hot, soapy water) all utensils that have touched raw meat.

- Keep drippings from raw meats away from other food.
- Disinfect surfaces after contact with raw meat or juice from meat.
- Rinse fruits and vegetables thoroughly before eating or cooking them. To rid them most effectively of germs and pesticide residue, wash them in a pint of water with a few drops of dishwashing soap added; rinse thoroughly.

### COOKING

*Cook to these internal temperatures:*
- Beef, veal, lamb (steaks and roasts): 145°F (63°C)
- Fish: 140°F (60°C)
- Ground beef: 160°F (72°C)
- Poultry: 180°F (83°C)
- Pork: 160°F (72°C)

### SERVING AND STORING

- Wash in hot, soapy water any utensils that were used in preparing food before using them to serve food.
- Eat hot food while it is still hot; eat cold food while it's still cold.
- Refrigerate leftovers immediately.
- Date leftovers and use them promptly; if in doubt about freshness, discard.

# CHILDPROOFING

## KEEPING KIDS SAFE AROUND THE HOUSE

CHILDREN HAVE A WAY OF FINDING HAZARDS YOU MIGHT NEVER HAVE SUSPECTED WERE THERE. IF KIDS LIVE IN YOUR HOME OR VISIT IT OFTEN, TAKE THESE PRECAUTIONS TO HELP KEEP THEM OUT OF HARM'S WAY.

### BATHROOMS

☐ Pad the bathtub spout.

☐ Place nonskid appliqués in the tub.

☐ Lock the medicine cabinet.

☐ Put cabinet locks on lower cabinets.

☐ Request child-resistant tops for prescription medicines.

☐ Keep razors well out of reach.

☐ Use a toilet-lid lock.

☐ Remove soaps small enough to fit into a child's mouth.

### BEDROOMS

☐ Keep beds and chairs away from window blinds and drapery cords.

☐ Remove breakable knickknacks.

### LIVING ROOM

☐ Pad sharp edges on furniture and raised fireplace hearths.

☐ Place nonskid backing on area rugs.

☐ Secure bookcases to the wall.

☐ Remove rickety furniture.

### KITCHEN

☐ Turn pot handles toward the back of the stove top.

☐ Keep knives and other sharp implements out of children's reach.

☐ Store plastic bags high and out of sight.

☐ Install latches on cabinets.

☐ Latch the refrigerator door.

☐ Remove small refrigerator magnets (they're choking hazards).

☐ Lock up trash containers.

☐ Store cleaning products in out-of-reach cabinets.

☐ Don't use tablecloths.

### THROUGHOUT THE HOUSE

☐ Install window guards (except on one window in each bedroom).

☐ Keep stairways clear; install gates at top and bottom.

☐ Keep furniture away from windows.

☐ Enclose the fireplace with glass doors.

☐ Cover electrical outlets with plastic plugs designed for the purpose.

☐ Keep wires, lamps, and lighting fixtures out of reach.

☐ Use sandwich bag ties or rubber bands to hold hanging cords out of reach.

☐ Make plants inaccessible to babies.

☐ Install sheets of rigid, clear plastic along stairway rails if they stand more than 4 inches (10cm) apart.

☐ Put decals on glass doors.

☐ Install knob covers on interior doors.

# WORKING WITH A DESIGNER

## CREATING A BETTER HOME BY DESIGN

———— ✳ ————

DOING YOUR HOMEWORK BEFORE YOU CALL A DESIGNER WILL HELP YOU PICK THE RIGHT PRO—IDEALLY, A PERSON WHOSE TASTES MESH WITH YOURS AND WHO IS WILLING TO WORK WITHIN YOUR BUDGET.

### BEFORE CALLING

- ☐ Start a project file.
- ☐ Decide on the rooms you want to do now—and later.
- ☐ List the activities that go on in each room.
- ☐ Create a list of styles you like and don't like.
- ☐ Clip and save appealing pictures from design magazines.
- ☐ Create a timetable.
- ☐ Ask friends for the names of designers.

### BEFORE HIRING

- ☐ Interview at least three designers.
- ☐ Take the time to look carefully at each designer's portfolio.
- ☐ Compare past work and budgets and make sure they're compatible with your plan. Choose the person with whom you are the most comfortable.

### BEFORE SPENDING

- ☐ Determine what you can afford to pay for the combination of furnishings, installation, and advice from a designer.
- ☐ Figure any structural improvements, such as refinishing floors or repainting walls, into the design budget.
- ☐ Comparison shop to get an idea of the market price of items, such as a new sofa or dining-room table, that you'll be adding to your home.
- ☐ Figure in the cost for a designer. The following are the most common ways in which designers and decorators bill for their services:

  *Cost-plus:* The designer buys materials, furnishings, and services at wholesale and sells to you at retail, pocketing the 15 to 20 percent difference as a fee.

  *Retail basis:* You buy the furnishings at market prices and pay the designer a percentage of the manufacturer's net cost as a fee.

  *Flat fee:* You pay the designer a fee agreed upon in advance to cover the job from design to installation.

  *Hourly charge:* A designer keeps track of time spent sketching, shopping, and supervising on your behalf; rates vary by service performed.

  *Design-with-purchase:* Buy furnishings from certain retailers, and they'll throw in design advice for free.
- ☐ Are you over budget before you've even started? Adjust your design in light of the costs you have identified.

# HIRING A HOUSECLEANER

## THINGS TO CONSIDER BEFORE SIGNING UP

---　＊　---

Be careful you don't get taken to the cleaners by a company with a spotty track record. Ask these questions and follow these steps before signing on with the housecleaner of your choice.

### WHEN CHOOSING A CLEANER

*Make sure you ask these questions:*

◆ What is and is not included in your basic cleaning service?

◆ What training do your employees have?

◆ Do you have references I may call?

◆ Are your employees bonded?

◆ Do you have a copy of your proof of liability insurance for my files?

◆ May I see a list of your cleaning procedures and products?

◆ Will you use cleaning products that are less toxic to kids, pets, and so on?

◆ Will you pay for the supplies?

◆ Will you give me a written cost estimate?

◆ What are the names of the employees who will be coming to my home?

◆ Do I need to be home when they arrive and while they are working?

◆ Will the same person or team clean my apartment or house each week?

◆ If I give you a house key, what safeguards do you follow to restrict its use?

◆ What is your cancellation policy?

◆ When do you expect payment?

◆ What happens if I'm not satisfied?

◆ What procedures do I follow if filing a claim for missing or damaged property?

### BEFORE CLEANERS ARRIVE

◆ Put away delicate, breakable objects and tuck any valuables safely out of sight of the cleaners.

◆ Put clutter away—if you're paying hourly, why should you pay the cleaner to move your things?

### AFTER THE JOB IS DONE

◆ Inspect the work within 24 hours.

◆ If you have any complaints, convey them to the company immediately.

# HIRING A CARPET CLEANER

## MAKING SURE THAT EVERYTHING'S COVERED

---※---

DON'T GET SWEPT UNDER THE RUG BY A CARPET CLEANER. MAKE SURE YOU ASK THE RIGHT QUESTIONS AND CHECK REFERENCES BEFORE AGREEING TO HAVE WORK DONE. ACT QUICKLY AFTERWARD IF THERE ARE PROBLEMS.

### WHEN CHOOSING A CLEANER

*Get answers to these questions:*

◆ Do you charge extra to move furniture?

◆ How long until I can walk on the carpet?

◆ Will fumes be a problem for seniors, children, pets, or people with allergies?

◆ Will you give me a written cost estimate?

◆ Do you have references I may call?

◆ Do you have a copy of your proof of liability insurance for my files?

### BEFORE CLEANERS ARRIVE

◆ Banish kids, pets, and houseplants from the areas to be cleaned.

◆ Remove breakable and valuable items.

◆ Put clutter away. Clear knickknacks off furniture that the carpet cleaners will be moving.

### AFTER THE JOB IS DONE

◆ Inspect the work within 24 hours.

◆ If you have complaints, make them known to the company immediately.

Feeling overwhelmed?
A cleaning pro can save the day.

# Basic Tools

———— ✳ ————

WHETHER IT'S A FAUCET THAT DRIPS OR A DOOR WITH A SQUEAKING HINGE, LITTLE PROBLEMS AROUND THE HOUSE ARE EASIER TO FIX WHEN YOU HAVE THE RIGHT TOOLS AND SUPPLIES ON HAND.

## ESSENTIAL TOOLS

- ☐ Adjustable wrench
- ☐ Battery-operated stud finder
- ☐ Claw hammer
- ☐ Combination square
- ☐ Cordless drill
- ☐ Crosscut saw
- ☐ Drill bits
- ☐ Flashlight
- ☐ Hacksaw
- ☐ Heavy-duty extension cords
- ☐ Pliers, locking, needle-nose, standard slip-joint, tongue-and-groove (medium size) and wire-cutting
- ☐ Plunger
- ☐ Putty knife
- ☐ Screwdrivers, standard and Phillips head (large and small)
- ☐ Tape measure
- ☐ Torpedo level
- ☐ Utility knife
- ☐ Utility light

## TOOLS FOR OCCASIONAL USE

- ☐ Circular saw, electric
- ☐ Clamps
- ☐ Drop cloths
- ☐ File
- ☐ Keyhole saw
- ☐ Lamp, clamp-on
- ☐ Paintbrushes
- ☐ Paint roller and tray
- ☐ Saber saw, electric
- ☐ Sander, electric palm or orbital
- ☐ Tack hammer
- ☐ Vise
- ☐ Wire brush
- ☐ Wrenches, crescent and socket

## SUPPLIES

- ☐ Caulk
- ☐ Cup hooks
- ☐ Duct tape
- ☐ Glue
- ☐ Graphite lock lubricant
- ☐ Liquid drain opener
- ☐ Lubricating oil
- ☐ Masking tape
- ☐ Nails and tacks
- ☐ Nuts and bolts
- ☐ Penetrating oil
- ☐ Picture hooks
- ☐ Rags, paper towels
- ☐ Sandpaper, coarse and fine
- ☐ Screws
- ☐ Spackling compound
- ☐ Washers, rubber and metal
- ☐ Wood putty

# SERVICE PROFESSIONALS

## MAINTENANCE AND REPAIR PROVIDERS

———— ✳ ————

B Y KEEPING A LIST OF REPAIR AND MAINTENANCE PROFESSIONALS WHOM YOU HAVE USED IN THE PAST—OR WHO HAVE BEEN REFERRED TO YOU—YOU CAN QUICKLY SOLVE PROBLEMS AS THEY COME UP.

### INTERIOR

Carpet cleaners_____

_____

_____

Handypersons_____

_____

_____

Housecleaning services_____

_____

_____

Locksmiths_____

_____

Pest control companies_____

_____

_____

### EXTERIOR

Chimney sweeps_____

_____

Lawn and landscape specialists_____

_____

Painters_____

_____

_____

Roofers_____

_____

Window washers_____

_____

### APPLIANCES AND SYSTEMS

Air-conditioning specialists_____

_____

Appliance repair services_____

_____

_____

Electricians_____

_____

Heating specialists_____

_____

_____

Plumbers_____

_____

_____

### OTHERS

_____

_____

_____

# HOME REPAIR HISTORY

## REPAIR AND MAINTENANCE LOG

— ✳ —

FOR A QUICK REFERENCE ON PAST HOME MAINTENANCE AND REPAIRS, FILL IN THE NAME OF THE COMPANY THAT PROVIDED EACH SERVICE, A DESCRIPTION OF THE WORK, AND THE DATE AND COST OF THE PROCEDURE.

*Interior*

### HEATING SYSTEM

Service_____

Vendor_____

_____

Date_____

Cost_____

### COOLING SYSTEM

Service_____

_____

Vendor_____

_____

Date_____

Cost_____

### ELECTRICAL WIRING

Service_____

_____

Vendor_____

_____

Date_____

Cost_____

### PLUMBING

Service_____

_____

Vendor_____

_____

Date_____

Cost_____

### CARPETS AND FLOORS

Service_____

_____

Vendor_____

_____

Date_____

Cost_____

### PAINTING AND WALLPAPER

Service_____

_____

Vendor_____

_____

Date_____

Cost_____

### OVEN AND STOVE TOP

Service_____

_____

Vendor_____

_____

Date_____

Cost_____

### DISHWASHER

Service_____

_____

Vendor_____

_____

Date_____

Cost_____

**REFRIGERATOR**

Service_____

_____

Vendor_____

_____

Date_____

Cost_____

**WASHER AND DRYER**

Service_____

_____

Vendor_____

_____

Date_____

Cost_____

*Exterior*

**ROOF**

Service_____

_____

Vendor_____

_____

Date_____

Cost_____

**CHIMNEY**

Service_____

_____

Vendor_____

_____

Date_____

Cost_____

**DOWNSPOUTS AND GUTTERS**

Service_____

_____

Vendor_____

_____

Date_____

Cost_____

The answer to your problem
is just a phone call away.

**LOCKS AND SECURITY**

Service_____

_____

Vendor_____

_____

Date_____

Cost_____

**PAINTING**

Service_____

_____

Vendor_____

_____

Date_____

Cost_____

**GARAGE DOOR**

Service_____

_____

Vendor_____

_____

Date_____

Cost_____

**LAWN AND LANDSCAPING**

Service_____

_____

Vendor_____

_____

Date_____

Cost_____

# RESOURCES

NEED MORE DETAILS? HERE ARE PUBLICATIONS, ORGANIZATIONS, AND SERVICES THAT OFFER INFORMATION AND SUPPLIES TO HELP YOU ORGANIZE, OUTFIT, CLEAN, AND MAINTAIN YOUR HOME.

## PUBLICATIONS

**All the Dirt on Cleaning**
The Soap and Detergent
Association
475 Park Avenue South
New York, NY 10016
(212) 725-1262
www.sdahq.org
*Write for this free 16-page guide
to choosing and using household
cleaning products—or pay a visit
to the Web site.*

**Amana's Guide to Cleaning
Appliances**
Amana Consumer Information
P.O. Box 8901
Amana, IA 52204
(800) 843-0304
*Send $3 postage and handling
for this 21-page booklet.*

**Carpet Care and Maintenance
for Maximum Performance**
The Carpet and Rug Institute
P.O. Box 2048
Dalton, GA 30722-2048
(800) 882-8846
www.carpet-rug.com
*Send an SASE to the address above
for a copy of this useful brochure.
For spot-removal advice, call or
visit the Web site.*

**Consumer Reports magazine**
(800) 234-1645
www.Consumer-Reports.org
*Consumer Reports gives impartial
critiques and testing of products.*

**House Beautiful magazine**
(515) 282-1508
www.housebeautiful.com
*Monthly publication offers decorating and shopping tips, and features
on the latest interior design trends
and furnishings. Visit the magazine's
Web site for additional ideas.*

**Today's Homeowner magazine**
(800) 456-6369
www.todayshomeowner.com
*For the home handyperson, expert
advice and detailed information
about home improvement and
repair, along with tips for outfitting your home.*

**The ULS Report**
P.O. Box 130116
Ann Arbor, MI 48113
http://cygnus-group.com/ULS
info@cygnus-group.com
*ULS stands for "use less stuff." This
bimonthly newsletter is published
by Partners for Environmental
Progress. Available free to consumers
by e-mail or at the Web site.*

## SUPPLIERS

**Hard-to-Find Tools catalog**
Brookstone Company
17 Riverside Street
Nashua, NH 03062
(800) 926-7000
www.brookstoneonline.com
*The Brookstone catalog offers unique
products and tools that range from
an air-blast drain gun to fanciful
mantel decorations.*

**Healthy Home catalog**
960C Harvest Drive
Blue Bell, PA 19422
(800) 394-3775
www.intellihealth.com
*Health-care products for allergy
relief, family health and safety,
and pain and stress relief.*

**Home Trends catalog**
1450 Lyell Avenue
Rochester, NY 14606-2184
(716) 254-6520
*Products for simple, effective
home cleaning, organizing,
and maintenance.*

**Hold Everything catalog**
Mail Order Department
P.O. Box 7807
San Francisco, CA 94120-7807
(800) 421-2285
*Creative, attractive products for
maximizing space all over the
house, and for displaying household
and personal items.*

**Home Decorators Collection
catalog**
8920 Pershall Road
Hazelwood, MO 63042-2809
(800) 245-2217
*Chairs, stools, lighting, contemporary furniture, rugs, outdoor
accents, and much more.*

**Kitchen & Home catalog**
P.O. Box 2527
La Crosse, WI 54602-2527
(800) 414-5544
*A mail-order source of innovative,
functional items for cooking and
beautiful living.*

*Solutions* catalog
P.O. Box 6878
Portland, OR 97228-6878
(800) 342-9988
*A collection of products designed to help organize and beautify your home and your life.*

## ORGANIZATIONS

**American Horticultural Society**
7931 East Boulevard Drive
Alexandria, VA 22308-1300
(703) 768-5700
http://members.aol.com/
gardenahs
*The society answers gardening questions by phone via its gardener's information service, Monday through Friday, 11 A.M. to 3 P.M. Eastern time. Or you can visit the group's Web site.*

**American Society of Interior Designers**
608 Massachusetts Avenue NE
Washington, DC 20002
www.interiors.org
(800) 775-2743
*Phone, write, or visit the Web site of the American Society of Interior Designers to find a designer in your area who has met the society's rigorous standards.*

**Food Marketing Institute**
800 Connecticut Avenue NW
Washington, DC 20006-2701
(202) 452-8444
www.fmi.org
*This food industry association provides information on safe food handling. Phone the office, or visit the Web site for links to other sources of food-related advice.*

**Interior Arrangement and Design Association**
1249 Peachtree Battle Avenue NW
Atlanta, GA 30327
(404) 352-0138
*Write for a designer in your area who can help rearrange what you own for a fresh new look—without your having to buy anything new.*

**National Association of Professional Organizers**
(512) 206-0151
www.ccsi.com/~asmi/napo.html
*To find a member in your area, call the local chapter or the national office, or visit the group's Web site.*

**National Burglar and Fire Alarm Association**
7101 Wisconsin Avenue, Ste. 901
Bethesda, MD 20814
(301) 907-3202
www.alarm.org
*Call or visit the Web site for a list of member companies in your area, or for a free copy of* Safe and Sound: Your Guide to Home Security.

**Paint and Decorating Retailers Association**
403 Axminster Drive
Saint Louis, MO 63026-2941
(314) 326-2636
www.pdra.org
*For cutting-edge decorating articles and answers to questions on remodeling and decorating, write or visit the nonprofit group's Web site.*

**National Gardening Association**
180 Flynn Avenue
Burlington, VT 05401
(800) 538-7476
www2.garden.org/nga
*This gardening organization offers answers to basic gardening questions on its Web site.*

**National Safe Kids Campaign**
1301 Pennsylvania Avenue NW,
Ste. 1000
Washington, DC 20004-1707
(202) 662-0600
www.safekids.org
*For family and child safety tips and strategies, call Safe Kids or visit its Web site.*

## OTHER RESOURCES

**Laura Ashley Home Styling Interior Design Service**
*This accessible in-home interior design service is available for $75, which includes decorating advice for up to two rooms. The fee is refundable with purchases over $750. To make an appointment for a designer to visit your home, call your local Laura Ashley store.*

**Mail Preference Service Direct Marketing Association**
P.O. Box 9008
Farmingdale, NY 11735-9008
www.the-dma.org
*To reduce the volume of unwanted mail, write to the association and request that your name and address be deleted from all mailing and marketing lists.*

**Ask Wisk Laundry Hotline**
Lever Brothers Company
Consumer Services Department
800 Sylvan Avenue
Englewood Cliffs, NJ 07632
(800) 275-9475
*Wisk sponsors this toll-free laundry question hotline from 8 A.M. to 6 P.M. Eastern time weekdays, and offers the* Ask Wisk Dirty Secrets, Clean Facts *brochure. Or you can write to the address above.*

# INDEX

Accident prevention, 45–47
Alarm systems, 105–107
Allergies, 38–39
Asbestos, 99
Bathrooms
  accidents in, 46–47
  caulking, 91–92
  cleaning, 39–40, 54, 59–61
  organizing, 22–23
  redecorating, 118
Bedrooms, 54, 119
Burglary prevention, 100–107
Carbon monoxide, 98
Carpets, 58, 62–63
Caulking, 91–92
Cleaning
  bathrooms, 39–40, 54, 59–61
  bedrooms, 54
  carpets, 58, 62–63
  clothes, 66–77
  dusting, 55
  finding time for, 32–34
  help with, 35–36
  kitchen, 40, 42, 54, 57–59
  products, 50–52, 53
  professionals, 65
  quick, 24, 61
  spring, 62–64
  techniques, 52, 55–64
  timetable, 54
Closets, 25–26
Clothes, 25–26, 66–77
Cooling system, 94–95
Decorative objects, 15, 116
Designers, 125–126
Doors, 102–103, 107
Energy conservation, 94–95
Fireplace, 81, 83, 109

Fire safety, 98, 99, 109
First aid, 98
Floors, 59, 63, 123–124
Food, 20, 21, 40–42
Furniture, 15–16, 55, 114–115, 120–121, 122
Gas, shutting off, 111
Glues, types of, 93
Health concerns, 37–42
Heating system, 83–84, 94
Home maintenance, 78–93
  emergency repairs, 88–90
  plumbing, 88–91
  preventive, 80–85
  timetable, 82
  tools for, 86–87
Home office, 28–29
Houseplants, 43–44, 116
Keys, 19, 103–104
Kids
  bedrooms for, 119
  cleaning and, 26–28, 35–36
  safety and, 45–47, 95
Kitchen
  accidents in, 46
  cleaning, 40, 42, 54
  energy savings in, 95
  organizing, 17, 19–22
  redecorating, 118–119
Laundry, 66–77
Lead paint, 99
Leaks, 84–85
Lights, 95, 104
Living room, 23–24, 46, 114–115
Locks, 103
Mail, 28, 29
Mildew, 42, 60, 84
Mirrors, 23, 55, 116
Natural disasters, 108–111

Organization, 10–29
  of papers, 28–29
  by room, 17–26
  starting, 12–15
Organizers, professional, 16
Oven, cleaning, 58
Paint, 99, 118
Parties, 127–128
Plumbing, 88–91
Radon gas, 99
Recipes, 20
Record-keeping, 28–29, 104
Redecorating, 112–126
Refrigerators, 64
Roof maintenance, 81
Safety and security, 96–111
  accidents, 45–47, 95
  burglaries, 100–107
  fire, 98, 99, 109
  first aid, 98
  hazardous substances, 99
  natural disasters, 108–111
  professionals, 106–107
Shelves, 15, 24
Silver, 55
Sinks, stopped-up, 89–90
Smoke detectors, 98
Stain removal, 63, 75–77
Storage, 14, 15, 18, 24–25
  of cleaning supplies, 53
  of food, 20, 21, 41
  for kids, 27
  of tools, 87
Toilets, 60, 88–89
Tools, 86, 87
Vacuuming, 39, 52, 55, 58, 64
Walls, 63–64, 92–93, 116
Water heater, 95
Weather stripping, 85
Windows, 55, 101–102, 106, 123

# ACKNOWLEDGMENTS

ADDITIONAL PHOTOGRAPHY: **Esto Photographics** 13 Peter Mauss; 17, 22, 33 Mark Darley; 39 Scott Frances. **FPG** 58 John Terence Turner; 60, 123 Stephen Simpson; 91 L'Image Magick Inc. **International Stock** 59 Scott Barrow; 121 Janis Schwartz. **Stock Market** 64 John Olson; 83 Gabe Palmer; 84 George Disario; 125 C/B Productions. **Tony Stone Images** 85 Chris Cheadle; 124 Guy Marche; 127 Zane Williams. **Jenny Thomas** 36, 73. **Uniphoto** 65 Frank Siteman; 74 Klaus Peter Wolf; 102 Ethel Davies; 110 Glenn Cormier. **Westlight** 34 Cydney Conger. Author photo by Brian Pierce. SPECIAL THANKS: The publishers wish to thank the following people for their valuable help during the creation of this book: Desne Border, Nancy Carlson, Rick Clogher, Mandy Erickson, Peggy Fallon, Barbara Hass, Ruth Jacobson, Esta Gallant Kornfield, Laurence Kornfield, Cynthia Rubin, Sharon Silva, Carrie Spector, Patrick Tucker, and Laurie Wertz for editorial assistance; Jan Collier for artist representation; Gigi Haycock for help with photo styling; Paul Rauschelbach for computing support; Sharon Smith for jacket design; Bill and Kristin Wurz for design assistance; Ken DellaPenta for indexing. Thanks also to the following sources for the loan of photographic props: Bette Kahn at Crate and Barrel (Northbrook, IL) and Ed Hoffacker at Palo Alto Sport Shop & Toy World (Palo Alto, CA). AUTHOR'S ACKNOWLEDGMENTS: I'd like to thank the following people for their help, support, and guidance, all of whom were instrumental in making this book simply a pleasure to write: Christopher Aronson, Connie Ballard, Rada Brooks, Phyllis Buvel, Kim Castagnola, Janet Goldenberg, Mark Hetts, and Shawna Kaylor.